Making External Experts Work

Making External Experts Work

Solutions for District Leaders

Thomas F. Evert and
Amy E. Van Deuren

ROWMAN & LITTLEFIELD EDUCATION
A division of
ROWMAN & LITTLEFIELD PUBLISHERS, INC.
Lanham • New York • Toronto • Plymouth, UK

Published by Rowman & Littlefield Publishers Education
A division of Rowman & Littlefield Publishing Group, Inc.
A wholly owned subsidiary of The Rowman & Littlefield Publishing Group, Inc.
4501 Forbes Boulevard, Suite 200, Lanham, Maryland 20706
http://www.rowmaneducation.com

Estover Road, Plymouth PL6 7PY, United Kingdom

Copyright © 2012 by Thomas F. Evert and Amy E. Van Deuren

All rights reserved. No part of this book may be reproduced in any form or by any electronic or mechanical means, including information storage and retrieval systems, without written permission from the publisher, except by a reviewer who may quote passages in a review.

British Library Cataloguing in Publication Information Available

Library of Congress Cataloging-in-Publication Data

Evert, Thomas F., 1947–
  Making external experts work : solutions for district leaders / Thomas F. Evert and Amy Van Deuren.
    p. cm.
  Includes bibliographical references.
  ISBN 978-1-61048-637-8 (cloth : alk. paper) — ISBN 978-1-61048-638-5 (pbk. : alk. paper) — ISBN 978-1-61048-639-2 (ebook)
  1. School superintendents—United States. 2. School districts—United States—Administration. I. Van Deuren, Amy, 1965– II. Title.
  LB2831.72.E93 2012
  371.2'011—dc23   2011039050

∞™ The paper used in this publication meets the minimum requirements of American National Standard for Information Sciences—Permanence of Paper for Printed Library Materials, ANSI/NISO Z39.48-1992.

Printed in the United States of America

Contents

A Note Regarding External Experts		vii
Preface *Tom Evert*		ix
Preface *Amy Van Deuren*		xiii
Chapter 1	External Experts: Overview and Context	1
Chapter 2	Creating Foundational System Change through Development and Adoption of a Decision-Making Model	29
Chapter 3	Addressing Diversity Issues in the District	61
Chapter 4	Using External Experts to Address a Wide Range of Issues	77
Chapter 5	Transferring and Implementing Proven Health Care Leadership Concepts to Public Education	97
Chapter 6	Lessons Learned about Leadership	111
References		131
Index		135
About the Authors		139

A Note Regarding External Experts

One of the first challenges in writing this book was to address the use of the term "consultant." It is not far-fetched to say that the term consultant has developed a negative connotation, especially in recent years. That is, when educators consider who consultants are and the value attached to them, the term often conjures up adjectives that create a stereotype, including "expensive, not connected, temporary, pie-in-the-sky" and more.

In preparation for teaching a doctoral course, we became aware of a new reference book on social media. Safko and Brake (2009) used the term "expert" instead of "consultant," and cited over twenty areas of expertise in the area of social media, including blogging, e-mail, podcasting, and search engines. Several chapters of Safko and Brake's book contain sections titled "Expert Insight." We believe that the terms "expert" and "external expert" positively capture the value that these individuals are capable of contributing to an organization. With this new sensitivity to the negative connotations associated with the term "consultant," the terms "expert" and "external expert" will be used throughout this book.

Preface

Tom Evert

During the years 1978–84, I had the opportunity to work with a progressive and forward-thinking superintendent in Beloit, Wisconsin, Dr. Mike Walls. In his work, Mike stressed the importance of reaching for new and worthwhile ideas regardless of the source. He also impressed upon me that in his work and experience with national consultants he came to the conclusion that most of these individuals were not only smart, innovative, and creative people; they were also good and caring people. I concur.

The turning point in my journey to seek the wisdom and direction of key consultants occurred after my first two years as superintendent. At that time, I was frustrated and restless, and I truly believed I was moving too slowly in my district leadership efforts. Fortunately, during the summer after my second school year was completed, I read the work of Jerry Patterson, educational administration professor, University of Alabama-Birmingham. Patterson had an excellent reputation as a change agent in the school districts of Madison and Appleton, Wisconsin. I expected to have my assessment of moving too slowly reinforced.

Surprisingly, I learned quite the opposite. According to Patterson (1993), systemic change takes 7 to 10 years in a school district, and while we can influence the growth curve, we cannot fundamentally change it. His observations, based on experience and research, provided me with the framework I needed to move forward with change. The framework included more closely observing the change process, seeking ideas from respective experts, and developing a willingness to help move the glacier known as the school district in a more directed, slow, and purposeful manner. In short, I settled in for the long haul and looked for ways to implement lasting, systemic change.

My work with the six external experts discussed in depth in this book provided many wonderful opportunities to develop and refine my strengths and talents as a district leader over my 14-year tenure as superintendent. I have a long-held fundamental belief that in order to be successful we must work to our strengths and minimize our weaknesses. The external experts in this book were not only able to analyze the district's problems and help develop and implement strategies for improvement, they were able to do so by helping me assess my strengths and weaknesses as a leader and encouraging forward movement based on such assessments. In short, each model forced me to think, dream, re-direct, and re-focus my approach to the superintendency, which in turn enabled me to do a better job for the district.

While this book is devoted to the work of a small handful of external experts used by one school district over a period of years, I would be remiss in not mentioning by name and saying a special "thank you" to other professionals who positively impacted my career. Their expertise has helped me in a variety of contexts, internal and external, traditional and non-traditional, and they have directly influenced my years in public education. Some of these people are individuals with whom I worked daily in the same school district over a number of years and who greatly influenced my personal and professional growth and development. Others are university consultants/teachers/advisors who gave me the chance to broaden my perspective and awareness. Still others are influential colleagues who taught me many lessons in many ways.

It is important to acknowledge those individuals who have had a positive impact on your career. As would be true with any list of this type, these are examples of influential educators and countless others could be included. Every educator has a list of experts like mine, and I encourage you to contact the people on your list to recognize them and say thank you.

In my formal higher education training, I was fortunate to have excellent faculty who provided sound guidance and important lessons for me. In particular, Jane Mercer, sociologist from the University of California, Riverside taught me the importance of looking from outside to inside when studying systems. John Thurston, psychologist and professor, University of Wisconsin-Eau Claire taught me the importance of developing in-depth expertise in an area and following longitudinal trends, and a belief that young professionals can be competent and assertive. William Reynolds, professor, University of Wisconsin-Madison taught me the importance of dedication to a field of study and the importance of acceptance.

I worked for several superintendents who taught me the importance of being yourself and of defining your system and style, including Mike Walls, Beloit; Don Mrdjenovich, Janesville; and George Longo, Sheboygan. My colleague and wife, Bette Lang, is an outstanding principal and superintendent who has always promoted integrity and commitment. Several school principals from Beloit taught me many lessons that have helped to shape my work in education, including George Kolak, who taught me the importance of zest, and Barb Hickman, who modeled the lesson that all educators must believe that all students can learn. My dear friend, school psychologist, and administrator Dave Luebke constantly stressed the importance of caring for and respecting all students.

Several Janesville teachers were important in my development and in my decision making processes, including Ed Stried, who promoted teacher professionalism; Jane Thompson, who lived a mission of dedication to all cultures and the mission that students learn about global issues; and John Eyster, from whom I learned the importance of polite persistence when addressing political issues.

Janesville principals were instrumental in making the district a success and were great supporters of changes that were beneficial to students. Mike Kuehne was a great example of the importance of combining humor, wit, and wisdom to benefit students and staff. Kitty Grant was a example of the great impact that positive approaches and enthusiasm can have when addressing difficult issues.

Janesville directors were a constant source of support and good advice from necessarily different perspectives. Jean Allen, Donna Behn, Doug Bunton, Steve Johnson, Pat Meehan, Steve Salerno, and Gary Bursell were all integral pieces, each figuring out how to fit his or her expertise into the big picture of the district in the ways that would best benefit students, parents, and the community. Gary Bursell in particular lived the importance of knowing when to be zany and why loyalty matters.

As a final thought, I have long been a proponent of system approaches and analysis since working with a consulting child psychiatrist, Dr. Harry Kniaz, in the 1970s and '80s. Harry was a thorough and competent diagnostician of child and adolescent psychiatric disorders and an excellent medical specialist focusing on systemic treatment plans, including the use of medications. However, what I learned the most from our twelve-year working relationship as psychiatrist and administrator/educational psychologist was his belief in analyzing systems: family systems, school systems, medical systems, community mental health systems, and so on in order to best serve others. That is, Harry was always looking at how parts affect the sum and how the sum affects the parts. I believe that district leaders are constantly applying such analysis in all aspects of their role and responsibilities. I also believe that it is frequently necessary for such analysis to include a completely external view or model as well as an analysis of how such a model could affect a school district. Ultimately, it is about staying current and keeping an open mind so that the best opportunities can be realized in the district.

Preface

Amy Van Deuren

In 2007, I was a new board member in a district facing significant budget reductions, and I was initially appalled when I found out the fees that were being charged by some of the external experts that had worked with the district in previous years. Even though these costs were typically not published in the local newspaper, I still felt it was my responsibility as a board member to curtail unnecessary district spending and keep as much money flowing directly into classrooms in the form of teaching staff and materials as possible. It seemed almost a sign of weakness that the district could not figure out how to solve some of these issues with which it struggled without this expert help.

In addition, any time the district brought in an external expert, it inevitably meant more meetings and time commitments for the board, and often it seemed as if the arrival of an external expert meant that we as a board somehow had less control over district direction. Sometimes it felt like the expert was being brought in to convince us as a board to adopt a district position, or to take a direction we were not inclined to take. So it was with great skepticism and mistrust that I initially viewed the subject of external experts. As I reflect back, I realize that part of this mistrust and skepticism was the result of being inexperienced as a board member coupled with the political mindset that I developed while running for public office. I am sure that my law background did not help my level of skepticism, either!

What I failed to understand at the time was that the district with which I was familiar did not get the way it was overnight. Despite the looming budget problems (which were affecting most of the districts in our state due to the state school funding system) our district was fiscally responsible and stable and was doing some things very well to provide many of the children of our community with an excellent education. I knew I felt good about sending my child to public school, a sentiment that my siblings in urban areas in other parts of the country could not share. I believed that the district had hired knowledgeable, professional teachers and staff, and my experiences participating in district meetings and functions during the campaign season left me with the impression that the district as whole was working hard to make an excellent learning environment even better for students.

I began to realize that one of the key reasons that the district was experiencing a high level of success was that district personnel demonstrated their own commitment to learning by themselves being lifelong learners. As such, district leadership brought in external experts not only to support and advocate for what they believed was right for students but to explore new ideas and approaches to do the very best job possible of serving all students. I began to appreciate the experts' ideas for direction, forums for discussion, and solutions that the external experts provided, and to value the questioning and debate that often surrounded the issues they were hired to address. I came to welcome the learning and insights that were gained by both the board and the administration as a result of interactions with external experts, and I firmly believe that the district was better for it.

During my one-year tenure on the board, I came into contact with four of the six external experts discussed in this book. Three of the experts I had the opportunity to work with closely, both as a board member and later as a grant evaluator and parent representative. I had very different experiences and received different insights from each of them and learned a great deal. While these individuals were not the only experts with whom I had contact, they represent a good cross-section of the types of situations in which experts were hired. In addition, as Dr. Evert and I discussed the topic of external experts in general, these six individuals kept coming up in conversation as excellent examples of successful engagements with external experts, and their stories and our different perspectives and experiences with these individuals continued to provide us with new insights about their roles, purposes, and effectiveness.

While the politics of board service was not without significant tension, discomfort, questioning, and stress, the atmosphere in the district office was charged with good energy and a sense of purpose and urgency toward ensuring that the district provided the most progressive and high-quality education it could to its students. External experts, used with purpose and discretion, helped district personnel maintain that energy, urgency, and focus on direction. As a result, many good things continued to happen for students in the district during my tenure on the board and beyond. I cannot thank teachers, administrators, support staff and other district personnel enough for what they do every day for my child and all the children of the district.

Chapter 1

External Experts

Overview and Context

There is nothing magical about a district leader working with and learning from any particular expert or combination of experts. Each school leader should choose experts based on what the district needs, what the expert offers, and the effectiveness with which the expert, district leadership, and the district stakeholders can work together to achieve the desired outcomes. The key components of this process include careful selection of external resources, purposeful gathering and study of data throughout the process, and monitoring progress as the work moves forward, while making any necessary adjustments along the way.

District leaders inevitably face significant challenges, especially when it comes to making large-scale, lasting changes in the district, addressing particularly difficult issues, or filling in the gaps when a particular area of expertise is required. A variety of internal and external resources are necessary in order to deal effectively with these challenges. While significant economic and political incentives often encourage school leaders to implement changes using exclusively internal resources (often overtaxing them), large-scale systems changes, difficult issues, professional development, grant-funded initiatives, and other undertakings can sometimes be moved forward most successfully by bringing in external experts.

The benefits of external experts varies. At the very least, these experts can provide a fresh perspective, with new ideas, direction and guidance regarding the issue(s) at hand. Ideally, these experts provide new insights, strategies, and action plans that move the district forward more successfully than could be accomplished without their input.

School district leaders are decision makers who face ongoing responsibility and accountability for student learning and achievement. A wide variety of short-term and long-term problems and dilemmas inevitably arise within every district and efforts should be made to successfully address them. Solutions to district dilemmas may be obtained from a variety of sources or combination of sources, including external experts. The savvy district leader understands his or her own knowledge, experience, strengths, and limitations, regardless of a district's size, location, wealth, culture, or politics. This district leader seeks ideas and services from as many internal and external experts as the circumstances dictate and resources allow.

This book is intended to provide district leaders at all levels with insight about why they should seek information, knowledge, and wisdom from a wide range of experts, specifically external experts, and how to make informed decisions about which external experts to use and when to use them. After all, the reality is that many external experts require a significant financial investment by the district. However, engaging external experts can be a judicious use of funds and create great value for districts at a time of fiscal constraints that may often include staff layoffs, especially at central office.

Ultimately, it is the responsibility of the district leader to ensure that the funds used for external experts results in maximum benefit to the district. Fulfilling this responsibility requires an understanding of the district's needs and openness to change, and the ability to acquire and use the right external expert for the situation at hand. This book describes various contexts and applications in which external experts have been successfully engaged. We believe that sharing these stories and lessons learned will prove insightful to readers.

This book utilizes a case study approach (Burke, 2009; Creswell, 2009), using the district as the case, and is based on the work of six experts and one superintendent in a medium-sized district of approximately 10,000 students with a long history of stable leadership and respectful, productive superintendent-board of education relationships. This history of stability and the authors' roles as long-standing superintendent and short-term board member provided an opportunity to experience, describe, and record the changes made in a district with consistent board and superintendent leadership over time.

The materials used in research for this work included extensive reviews of notes and records, including board meeting minutes, and other district documentation. During the time frame covered in this book, the district environment was such that the board of education and the superintendent encouraged the implementation of new ideas and there were many considerations of large and small district-wide changes that would benefit students.

Practical application in mind, this book is written from the perspective of a veteran superintendent (also high school principal, director of student services, private therapist, and school psychologist) and a former board of education member (also attorney, high school teacher, small business owner, and author of education reference books).The writers' different perspectives and their own interactions with the experts discussed in this book are intended to offer readers an unique lens through which to view and consider the subject of external consultants. Ultimately, it is hoped that district leaders at all levels can benefit from the experience and expertise that has been recorded, organized, analyzed, and synthesized in this book.

ABOUT THE DISTRICT

The experts discussed in this book worked in a mid-size district in a city with a general population of about 60,000 and a student population of about 10,000. The city is located in a Midwest state known for its dedication to excellent pre K-12 public schools. This district is unique in its "averageness." That is, as a medium-sized school district in a medium-sized city, it boasts an average income near the state average and a population whose demographics approximate state average numbers. However, one area where this district is *not* average is in the length of tenure that previous superintendents have enjoyed. In a span of over 70 years from 1935 to 2008, only four superintendents served the district. In a profession with an average tenure of approximately three years at any one school district, this statistic is truly remarkable. So, too, are the arguable results of this statistic: a district with substantial leadership longevity and the ability to implement a vision consistently over time.

The district currently consists of twelve elementary schools, three middle schools, two high schools, and five charter schools. In addition, in 2007 the board approved a four-year-old kindergarten model that partnered with area day care providers to offer the program in the day care facilities. The community has a long history of supporting the school district, passing several major facilities referendums in the time period covered in this book, most notably a building referendum that was the largest in the state at the time of passage. Facilities were built and/or updated and regularly maintained, keeping pace with need during times of population growth.

The experts discussed in this book were hired over a 12-year period, and represent a wide variety of needs that an expert may be hired to address. The superintendent under which these external experts were hired had several advantages: (1) he had worked in the district for some time before becoming superintendent (familiarity with the district); (2) he had access to the recently retired long-standing superintendent who remained in the area; and (3) he had time to learn the district from the superintendent's lens in order to make savvy decisions about when and for what an external expert would be beneficial to the district.

In addition to stability in the superintendency, there was also a great deal of stability in the next level of line authority, the directors. The district employs four directors in the areas of Human Resources, Finance, Student Services, and Curriculum and Instruction. Two of these four directors were in their positions before the superintendent was hired, and these two individuals remained in the district until the end of the superintendent's tenure with the district. One of the other directors had significant leadership experience in this and nearby districts, and the last director had previous experience as a director in another district. This talented group functioned well together as a team, each director clear in his or her roles and responsibilities. Each brought the perspective of his or her area to the discussion at hand, and all were open to learning from both internal and external sources.

AN OVERVIEW OF RESOURCES FOR SCHOOL DISTRICTS

There is no question that district leaders should consider several factors when deciding whether to engage an external expert, including accessibility, availability, quality, and cost. Although this book focuses on a handful of external experts, it is beneficial to briefly discuss other external resources that may or may not be quite so obvious to the busy district leader. By no means is the focus of this book on external resources intended to marginalize the value of the extensive resources available internally in most districts. Many dedicated education professionals devote a great deal of time to their assigned duties and many take on other additional duties as well in order to make the district a better place for student learning. However, the reality is that these individuals are often stretched thin, and may or may not possess the full range of expertise often required to take on specific tasks and challenges.

In addition, a great deal of current writing focuses on maximizing the use of the internal resources in a district (Calhoun, 1994; DuFour & Berkey, 1995; Haslam, 1997; Wong, 2002). We fully acknowledge the value of these internal resources; however, we contend that districts should also consider the perspectives of those who are not involved in the daily operations of the schools. Sometimes a fresh look, new ideas, and alternative approaches can energize a district and help facilitate positive change.

Some external resources may be available at low or no cost. Useful resources are publicly funded or privately funded community organizations, such as civic and service clubs, churches, physicians, attorneys, county mental health services, police and fire departments. District leaders who

Table 1.1. External Experts Location/Funding Matrix

	Local Community Experts	Outside of Community Experts
Privately Funded	• Accountants • Attorneys • Chamber of Commerce • Churches • Contractors • Physicians • Service clubs (Rotary, Lions, Knights of Columbus, etc.)	• Carol Wirth • Dr. Golarz • Dr. Odom • Ken Trump • Specialized Attorneys • Wm. Strauss
Publically Funded	• County mental Health • District Attorney • Fire • Local colleges • Police • Social Services	• Federal Department of Education • Intermediate agencies • Professional Organizations • Research Universities • State Department of Education
Volunteer/Donation	• Parents • Local Businesses	• Studer Group

*While professional organization memberships are the responsibility of individual members, these memberships are typically negotiated as part of a professional contract and paid out of district funds.

effectively cultivate relationships with these groups can find them of great value to the district, sometimes in unexpected ways. Table 1.1 represents one way of considering a wide range of experts according to how they are funded and whether or not they are available locally.

Local community experts can serve a wide variety of needs in the district. Perhaps the greatest advantages of local community experts are their availability and their knowledge of the community. That is, these resources are readily available for regular communication, including formal and informal consultation, brainstorming, and feedback. Typically, these resources are familiar with the culture and political climate of the community and the school district, saving the district time and money because they already possess extensive background and context.

These local community experts may be used in a variety of district contexts, situations, and implementations. A few examples include advising on referendums, consulting about the effects of operational changes on the community, and helping the district celebrate student, school, and district successes. Some local community experts are already fixtures in the district, most notably local attorneys, who are typically brought in when needed.

While attorneys and other specialized resources charge a fee, typically their fees will be less than the fees of experts outside of the community, and they will not require travel, lodging, and/or meal expenses.

External resources (outside of the community) can be an important component of addressing urgent, difficult, and/or specialized district needs. They often offer expertise that simply cannot be found locally. They can help districts navigate through difficult territory, often providing very specialized knowledge in a narrow subject area, new and valuable insights and information, new approaches to large or ongoing problems, or a neutral voice in addressing a sensitive or controversial issue. For example, the University of Wisconsin-Madison Center for Applied Population Analysis provides school districts typically throughout the state with in-depth enrollment projections for a very reasonable fee.

Publicly Funded Local Experts

District leaders frequently find it helpful to develop district partnerships with a variety of publicly funded local organizations, including local police and fire departments, charitable and civic organizations, and local colleges. Some of these organizations will have relationships with the district as a matter of health and public safety, such as the fire and police departments; however, others mentioned above may be somewhat less recognized but still very important. These organizations generally incur little or no cost to districts, and districts can effectively partner with these organizations to develop and promote initiatives that benefit both organizations. Partnering with local organizations also adds strength in numbers to the undertaking and often results in increased community support. Sharing ideas and resources with publicly funded local community experts and organizations can help all the partnership organizations provide better, more efficient, and more cost-effective services to the community.

For example, the district discussed in this book and a neighboring district engaged in a partnership with county police, fire department, sheriff's department, district attorney's office, and social services to improve emergency preparation between these organizations. As a result, safety training and drills in both district schools are now improved to a degree well above the state-mandated minimums. Police and fire departments have better documentation on each school building and members of all organizations have a high level of clarity on the protocol of communication and action in the event an emergency incident occurs, large or small. As a result of these efforts, all organizations respond more efficiently and effectively in an actual emergency situation.

Publicly Funded Experts Outside the Community

Publicly funded experts are readily available outside of the local community. State and federal agencies, including the U.S. Department of Education and state Departments of Education provide a plethora of helpful information and services. These departments and other governmental agencies are staffed with a variety of knowledgeable and experienced individuals who can provide direction and guidance (or at least a starting point) on many issues. A phone call or e-mail to individuals in these organizations can often yield helpful information and suggestions regarding next steps. Many states also have an intermediate agency that bridges the gap between the state agency and local school district.

For example, the Cooperative Educational Service Agency (CESA) in Wisconsin is an intermediate agency with regional offices throughout the state. CESA is funded partly by local districts utilizing their services and the organization also receives significant state funds and categorical grant aid. CESA is able to offer cooperative services to districts, often at a lower cost to the district than they would incur had they obtained those services on their own. CESA provides a wide variety of special education services, and services in areas such as technology, gifted and talented, and school improvement.

Research universities throughout the country can be excellent resources, especially if the district can locate a department or team conducting research or considering new approaches to problems and issues that face the district. For example, if the district is facing significant problems with truancy, seeking a research university where one or more students is studying new approaches to reducing truancy can provide the district with a new way of addressing the issue. This arrangement is also beneficial to universities, because the school district provides researchers with appropriate populations on which to test their theories and approaches.

Two-year universities and technical colleges should not be overlooked, either, as valuable resources to a public school district. For example, when a district charter school housed in a non-district owned location was facing closure due to lack of funding, the local two-year university stepped in and offered classroom space. This accommodation was made largely because the district had provided the university with space for a major project in the past. The collaborative relationship served each organization well and allowed each to accomplish goals it could not otherwise have accomplished.

Privately Funded Local Experts

Privately funded local experts can be a great asset to a community as well as a school district. Churches and service clubs sponsor programs for schools, give scholarships to students, and recognize outstanding student achievement.

They are focused on giving back to the community, and the benefits they provide to the district are usually significant. These organizations typically consist of members with strong opinions and beliefs about the community, and they can offer valuable insight on community perceptions. The members of these organizations are often civic-minded professionals who possess a wide range of abilities and expertise. Including these individuals in focus groups and brainstorming sessions can bring new ideas into the district and perhaps offer new insight to issues and problems facing the district.

Other privately funded local experts include professionals, who can provide necessary information and advice on specialized topics. These individuals often charge a fee for their services and may be retained by the district so that they are readily available when the need arises (particularly attorneys). However, private local experts are readily available in other capacities as well. For example, accountants can be engaged to provide costing estimates for insurance proposals from various providers. Using a bidding process for facilities construction and/or improvements is a way to get the input of a variety of local experts on what they believe a quality job should look like and how much it should cost.

Privately Funded Experts Outside the Community

Privately funded experts outside the community (external experts) are those that are often brought in to analyze or study a particular issue, solve a particular problem, or guide a new implementation or system. They are typically paid through district funds or grant funds. Sometimes, a district leader will have a discretionary budget from which he or she may hire an external expert on occasion, or the district leader may be required to seek Board approval for such expenditures.

While external experts can offer significant benefits to a district, especially when the district and the expert are a good match, external experts sometimes carry a negative stigma within the district and in the community. External experts usually require a financial investment, and are often described as being a one time proposition. That is, they come in, promote their agenda, impart information, perhaps generate some excitement, and then leave with questionable lasting impact. In some cases, a vendor pays an expert's fee and the costs of the presentation (and the expert) are not known until the sales pitch is made and a product purchased (which may or may not have lasting benefit to the district).

Some of this negative reputation is doubtless justified; however, many district leaders understand that external experts can be an important resource for district improvement. In addition, districts are finding ways to use external experts that positively impact the bottom line. That is, it is often more cost effective to bring in an external expert to address a specific, specialized issue than it is to hire a person as an employee to address the issue. Of course, the nature of the work to be done often dictates whether an external expert is an appropriate solution.

Volunteers/Donations/College Students

Sometimes, opportunities to bring an expert to the district may be a matter of the district's willingness to experiment. Experts who are trying new approaches or using techniques that work well in other fields may be willing to donate their time and expertise to see whether those approaches or techniques will work successfully in a public school setting. These experts may be external experts in a traditional sense, or may be parents or other community members with a vested interest in seeing the district succeed.

Recognizing good ideas and sound plans for implementation from these resources can be significantly more risky than engaging an experienced expert with a successful public school track record; however, it can also be a golden opportunity to benefit the district without the hefty price tag. Careful research, discussion, and planning with a variety of district stakeholders and the community is advised before engaging an expert who is willing to donate his or her services.

Student teachers and graduate students are also valuable resources. In addition to raising important questions about instructional and administrative practices and procedures, these individuals participate in applied research activities that can have direct benefit to the district. Efforts to develop partnerships with local colleges and universities can occur at the school or district level. Hosting student teachers can serve as valuable professional development opportunities for experienced teachers, and participating in various research efforts can offer unique insights into the district that might be difficult to obtain using other methods. While these contributions can vary greatly by district, their value should not be overlooked.

EXTERNAL EXPERTS: PRACTICAL CONSIDERATIONS

Why Consider an External Expert?

Before engaging in a lengthy discussion about external experts, perhaps it is worth deeper consideration regarding why one might be hired in the first place. After all, a savvy school leader with a supportive board, competent administrative team, and talented teachers should be able to address any issues or problems that arise, and this group of individuals will undoubtedly have no shortage of creative ideas for moving the district forward. Regardless how true this scenario may be, there are simply times when bringing someone in from the outside has benefits that drawing from within alone simply does not.

An external expert can create a new sense of urgency. By bringing in an external expert, the district makes a strong statement about the importance of the issue being addressed: The district is willing to invest resources to make improvements. An external expert can help internal audiences look at ongoing issues in new ways. An external expert does not have the political and personnel perspective that internal audience members may have. That is they are more free to "call it as they see it" and they do not have to fear the ramifications of their negative analysis the same way a board member or district employee would. Lastly, an external expert clearly understands that his or her role is temporary, even if the engagement spans several years.

Ward (2010) recommends seeking experts to work with district administrators over several years. Whether the engagement of the external is short term or long term, thinking of external experts as "targeted change agents" is a good way to frame their purpose and value. These targeted change agents can offer advice and analysis that employees of the district may not see or be comfortable articulating.

In 1984, English and Steffy identified five specific reasons why school districts look to external resources to fill certain needs: (1) Lack of technical expertise; (2) lack of independence or objectivity; (3) lack of political strength; (4) lack of vision; and (5) lack of credibility (pp. 3, 9). While these reasons are certainly legitimate when considering an external expert, the underlying message from English and Steffy is that districts hire external experts when they are *lacking* something. That is, when things are going *well enough*, leaders may perceive that external experts are not needed.

This approach encourages leaders to look at whether or not there are problems. In today's educational climate, the question should transcend this "problems" approach and become a question of whether or not things can be made even *better* than they are. Jim Collins' book *Good to Great* counters this problem-driven approach. Perhaps the recognition that *good* is not often *good enough* is the reason that Collin's work has resonated with so many people since its first publication in 2001, and why organizations begin to experience stagnation when they reach *good*.

Fast-forward 25 years. Ralph Heath (2009), former president of Ovation Marketing, discusses a different approach to external experts in his book *Celebrating Failure: The Power of Taking Risks, Making Mistakes, and Thinking Big*. Even though the context of his comments is business and not education, his perspective is still worth consideration for the school district leader. "When ... you can greatly improve the way people perform their jobs, then it only takes a small overall improvement on everyone's part to make the investment pay off in a huge way" (p. 127). To further elaborate on this approach, Heath relays the following story:

> An associate once asked me why I would spend money to bring in a consultant instead of putting money toward deserving staff salaries. . . . My associate thought that his own value was somehow diminished because I felt the need to spend money on a consultant to further develop his skills. Nothing could be further from the truth. Spending decisions should never be made in terms of money spent versus another person's salary. . . . We are aware that the . . . [money] we spend on a consultant will not be available for salaries—mine included—or any other expense for that matter. But that fact is not much more than a blip on the radar screen when deciding to make an investment in equipment, training, or people. (pp. 127–128)

What this associate failed to understand was that Heath was spending money on experts, not because he was not valued, but precisely because he was *so* highly valued that the company wanted him and other employees to continue on their successful path. Heath also believed it was important to ensure that the employees understood the thinking behind this investment. "A good open-book company will share the thinking behind the ROI numbers with its clients and its employees" (ROI = Return on Investment) (p. 130).

In the context of business, ROI generally refers to the impacts of money spent on the bottom line (profits). In education, the ROI is harder to define, but ultimately, any money invested should improve student achievement and learning on some level. Investing resources on opportunities that improve student achievement and learning, including the use of external experts, are arguably well-spent resources.

Heath's framework for considering external experts does not contradict nor in any other way negate English and Steffy's work. Rather, it expands the underlying message. Instead of resorting to an external expert only when there is a *lack,* Heath views resources spent on external experts as a valuable investment in raising the professional skill levels and performance of staff, making what is already working well work even better, improving alignment to and synchronization with organizational goals.

Education is a fluid profession. New curricula, programs, initiatives, government mandates, technologies, and educational theories are always emerging. This fluidity occurs not only from new research and design, but also in large part due to the ever-changing needs and dynamics of the students being taught. As a result, the need for school districts to stretch beyond "lack of" thinking to "good to great" thinking is more important today than ever. Broader consideration about when an external expert may be an investment versus a necessary evil to address a perceived lack may ultimately have better outcomes for the district when such an expert is hired.

There are many good reasons to consider hiring external experts as targeted change agents in a school district setting. Each school leader must consider for himself or herself whether or not a particular problem, issue, initiative, or change would benefit from the input, guidance, and direction of an external expert. Important factors, including time, expense, effort, and additional work must be carefully thought through before hiring an external expert. External experts can be very powerful tools in the arsenal of a district leader, and as targeted change agents, they can often help the district accomplish goals that would be extremely difficult to accomplish without them.

Limitations of Relying on Internal Resources—Politics and Time

The idea of maximizing expertise using internal resources within the district has gained popularity, reducing the perceived need for external experts. Instead of bringing in an external expert, hybrid models, such as "train the trainer" have been popular, where a handful of internal staff members are trained and then expected to pass on their new knowledge to others in the district. It is understandable why these approaches have gained popularity. Asking a board of education to approve the expenses associated with an external expert in a climate of increased need and less available funds can be challenging. Allocating funds in the yearly budget for such expenditures may not be as feasible as it once was. When districts invest in high-quality professional development for teachers and administrators, board members may believe that the district has adequate expertise in its internal audiences to completely fill whatever needs the district may have for experts.

Using internal resources to address district issues is not without substantial merit; however, internal resources alone may not be adequate to fully address the problems and issues, or successfully implement new programs and initiatives. Two important reasons for this inadequacy have virtually nothing to do with the internal resource's level of expertise per se. Districts are typically staffed with individuals who, as a whole, possess a great wealth of knowledge and expertise. Rather, it is the nature of being *internal* that causes potential limitations to the internal resource's ultimate ability to be effective as targeted change agents. These two limitations are politics (using the term broadly) and time.

Addressing some issues internally may have political ramifications that nullify or offset the expertise that the internal resources offer. Staff and other district personnel are affected by the culture and climate in a district, as well as by their status as an employee in the district and the implications thereof. For example, districts struggling with racial tension may well find themselves deeply divided in a "we-they" standoff if they try to address the issues internally. Negative effects may range from strained workplace environments to negative impacts on students to lawsuits. Sensitive issues that go to individuals' deep-seated beliefs might be best addressed by a neutral third party who is specifically trained to facilitate the process of lasting, meaningful change on such a divisive issue as race. Considering the risks of addressing an issue such as racial tension without help against the cost of hiring a competent, trained professional, suddenly the costs of the professional do not seem quite so high.

The other limitation when relying on internal resources in some matters is simply that of time. Perhaps the appropriate level of expertise is available in the district, but the person or people who possess the expertise also typically have a full plate of obligations and duties as part of their employment. That is, they simply cannot free up adequate time to do justice to another project or issue and still maintain their quality of work in their primary capacity. These individuals are often excellent resources and sounding boards, but sometimes, it is more efficient and cost effective to bring in an external expert to devote adequate time and focus on a particular issue, project, or implementation.

Funding an External Expert

Funding external experts is typically not given a great deal of focused attention in college and university administrative leadership training programs. Hoyle, Björk, Collier, and Glass (1997) indicate that issues superintendents must understand in relation to budgeting and finance are taxation systems, budget creation and management, and financial projections. A clear understanding of budget management and financial projections can help superintendents understand the best ways to fund external experts in their districts.

Although funds are available from many sources, it is easiest if the superintendent has a budgeted amount that he or she may allocate as needs arise for professional development and training throughout the district McCabe, Cunningham, Harvey, and Koff (2005) recommend that the district allocate a minimum of one percent of the budget toward professional development of some type (p. 90). At least some of this budget is often allocated for the superintendent to use at his or her discretion. However, several conversations with regional superintendents in the Midwest over many years reveals that superintendents are generally reticent to ask for such a departmental budget if one does not already exist. That is, asking for a discretionary department budget to be continued is far easier than asking for the creation of such a budget.

In the absence of a discretionary departmental budget, formal board approval for funding external experts will usually be necessary. Depending on the political climate and the reason the external expert is being sought, seeking formal board approval may strengthen or weaken community support for the hiring of the external expert. Regardless of whether or not formal board approval is required, it is imperative that there is adequate support for the hire of the external expert on the part of the board, the administration, and often several other stakeholder groups.

If the superintendent does not have funds to allocate for professional development and/or consultation, funds for external experts can come from other sources. Superintendents can and should consider private local sources for funding. The Westchester Institute for Human Services Research (1998) acknowledges that although "little information exists on how much states and school districts actually spend on staff development. . . . we do know from the research . . . that local districts bear most of the costs" (p. 2). Local Chambers of Commerce, business organizations, and philanthropists can be excellent resources for funding special expenditures that are perceived to provide important enhancement for schools.

Conducting general discussions about external experts with the board can help to determine an initial degree of board support for this type of resource. Such a discussion should candidly address the needs of the district that might be most effectively and efficiently served by an external expert. This discussion should also include a general cost/benefit analysis. That is, the cost of engaging an external expert should be compared to the costs (both direct and indirect) of achieving the similar results or obtaining similar services using other means, such as hiring staff, extending existing staff, or sending a group of staff members for training. Providing goal clarifications, cost/benefit analyses, and articulating the return on investment to the board and other stakeholders when discussing the possibility of using external experts places costs in an appropriate context.

Hiring an External Expert

It is important to understand what an external expert can and cannot do and when such a resource may be worth the effort and expense. Typically, an external expert does not relieve the district of the workload; far from it. Instead, he or she often *creates* a workload for the district in some manner. Typically, the expert has been in their field of expertise for many years, and possesses a great deal of knowledge and experience. In this sense, as far as *content* regarding the issue, the expert brings the expertise; that is why he or she is being hired.

The expert typically must work hard to learn the district, identify the issues, actively apply his or her knowledge and expertise to the issues to create viable, attainable solutions, and help guide the district through the implementation of those solutions. The district and the expert should work together to ensure that both parties understand the ends, the means, and the challenges. This cooperation increases the likelihood that the results desired for the district can be achieved in the manner the district expects and needs and that the expert can deliver.

The following list of questions for both the district and the expert are useful in determining whether an external expert should be considered for hire, and/or whether a particular expert is right for the job.

1. *Why is the expert being hired?* The district should be very clear about the issue the expert is being hired to address, and at least a core of district leaders (board, superintendent, directors) should be in some reasonable level of agreement that an external expert is the best way to address the issue. If the expert encounters tension regarding his or her engagement with the district, the task at hand becomes much more difficult, especially if the issue is a contentious one.
2. *What are the objectives that the district is trying to accomplish?* Just like a good lesson plan, clear objectives and specific goals will help keep both the district and the expert on track.
3. *What are the anticipated time frames for critical junctures?* It is important to establish critical junctures or specific checkpoints that are key to accomplishing the goals of the expert's engagement. In addition, tentative time frames for these critical junctures ensure that everyone understands the expectations for progress as the work moves forward. Using these time frames for critical junctures to monitor progress helps all stakeholders and the expert gauge how well the work is staying on its originally intended course.
4. *What are the anticipated costs to achieve these objectives?* Costs to achieve intended results are likely to extend beyond the fee of the external expert. It is important to consider all of the potential costs that may be associated with the work of the expert. Additional costs may include substitute teacher pay, supplies, materials, travel, and other costs.
5. *What are the methods and criteria that will be used to assess whether or not objectives have been accomplished?* The district should determine the methods and criteria for accountability that will used to assess the effectiveness of the external expert. These accountability measures

should be made clear to the external expert at the time of hire. If the district has flexibility on this matter, clarifying assessment methods and criteria in partnership with the external expert at the outset will ensure that the expectations for the engagement are clearly communicated to everyone.
6. *What types of documentation does the district expect from the expert?* It is not uncommon for experts to provide detailed assessments, reports, recommendations, data, and other materials as part of their services. It is a good idea to discuss and clarify expectations regarding the frequency, length, and detail of these documents in advance.

Clearly communicating expectations, both for outcome and process, can help make experiences with external experts more positive and productive for the district. If a formal hire is made, typically a formal contract will accompany the engagement. A formal contract will contain the terms of the engagement and other relevant issues (often both legal and practical) governing the relationship.

The Importance of External Experts for the District Leader's Professional Development

The superintendent's position is a lonely one. Superintendents do not expect teachers and administrators to improve their own job performance without spending district money on professional development, yet it seems to be the norm of expectation that superintendents should be able to perform to their maximum potential without such district support. Perhaps this phenomenon occurs because the superintendent is typically the most highly paid person in the district, and funding professional development on top of a high salary seems excessive.

Or perhaps superintendents are reluctant to spend district funds on their own professional development because the superintendent is an "n of one," and as such, it can seem rather selfish and/or self-serving to ask the board to approve funding for his or her own professional growth, especially if it is not negotiated in the initial hiring process. However, upon reflection, it is not difficult to understand why it is so important that the superintendent is provided with appropriate resources for professional development that will help him or her provide better overall leadership for the district.

A critical area in which the superintendent's position is an n of one is that of perspective. Often, public statements made by the board, parents, staff, or students reflect the sentiments of more than one person in the group; however, statements made by the superintendent reflect directly on him or her. It is critical that the superintendent's perspective align as much as possible with the values of the community, the board, and the staff in order for the superintendent to serve the school district effectively. Regardless of the level of superintendent involvement in various district activities, sometimes it is invaluable to have an external expert with no internal agenda weigh in with his or her observations and recommendations.

District leaders have a responsibility to the district and themselves to further and enhance their own professional development. Professional development is an important component of successful, sustained district leadership (AASA National Superintendent of the Year Forum). Effective professional development for district leaders can take many forms, including academic coaching, studying books and journals, and networking with other superintendents. University classes and professional development programs provide support and direction for leadership growth and improvement.

Professional development offerings cover a wide variety of topics, from the role of the superintendent to getting through the first year on the job. District leaders receive a plethora of information from state and national associations regarding training opportunities and resources to help them lead the district. The depth and breadth of this information and these opportunities can be overwhelming at times, and district leaders have difficult choices to make regarding how to best spend limited personal and professional time and funds for their own growth and development.

Sometimes, district leaders tend to overlook their own professional development as they become immersed in the daily operations and political arena of leadership. This tendency is understandable for several reasons:

1. *Time.* There simply are not enough hours in the day and night to do all of the leadership and management tasks associated with the superintendency. Attending board meetings and other evening functions in addition to full days can severely limit time to read, study, and consult with experts.
2. *Resources.* It is often much easier to justify spending district funds on staff professional development than on superintendent professional development. There seems to be something self-serving and inherently anti "servant leader" (Sergiovanni, 1996) about a superintendent advocating the investment of district funds in him or herself, especially in difficult economic times. It is much easier to funnel funds to staff professional development and other district needs, although it is every bit as important that the district leader receive professional development as it is for other staff members.

    Unfortunately, the reality is that the nature of that professional development for the district leader is likely to be very different from that of other staff. Because the superintendent is an n of one, his or

her professional development is likely to be more individualized and specialized than that of other district personnel.
3. *Determination of Need.* District leaders not only have the responsibility to obtain their own professional development, but they must also figure out what *it* is. While several good resources and opportunities exist, the superintendent must decide which to choose, and determine the potential for positive impact to the district as well as to self.
4. *Accountability.* If teachers or administrators receive professional development but certain individuals do not find it useful, it can still be deemed a success for the rest of the attendees. Even poorly rated professional development opportunities will usually contain at least something of value that make the effort worthwhile. However, if a superintendent invests time and money into a professional development opportunity, he or she may feel a heightened sense of responsibility to ensure that the investment is worthwhile, even if the professional development results in value that does not directly benefit the district.

That is, superintendents arranging their own professional development must take full ownership of the decisions made to attend conferences and classes or consult with experts. In addition, it is their responsibility to explain the expenditures and benefits of these activities to boards and constituents, and to prepare justifications for time away from district duties.

External experts can be an effective way for superintendents to obtain a more objective perspective than is likely to be found in the district, and receive personalized, meaningful professional development in the process as a collateral benefit of engaging in the process of district improvement. External experts can help the superintendent frame the challenges and issues in ways that provide direction for additional professional development opportunities and/or study. Many external experts are also an excellent resource for additional materials and opportunities for various stakeholders that might best enhance the work at hand. In short, an external expert can not only help the district move forward, he or she can also help the superintendent move forward to become a more effective leader for the district.

FEATURED EXTERNAL EXPERTS

This book focuses on the work and lessons learned from six external experts: Dr. Ray Golarz, Dr. John Odom, Mr. William Strauss, Mr. Quint Studer, Mr. Ken Trump, and Ms. Carol Wirth. In depth discussion of these experts includes the following four components: (1) the background, history, and chronology of the relationship between the expert and the district; (2) the story of the district's overall experience with the expert; (3) a discussion of the content the expert brought to the district and how it was helpful, and (4) the lessons learned from each expert. Each expert is presented from the perspectives of content, context, and process. Each expert made significant contributions to the district, and the influence of each one continues in some form today.

Each external expert has a unique story from which we can all learn. In a very real way, each external expert helped shape the history of the district, whether the impact affects the entire district or whether a specific, important piece of district was significantly affected. As a result of the influences of these experts, some important aspect of the district works better than it did before the expert left his or her mark. Sometimes, culture and climate are significantly altered as a result of the expert's work, requiring virtually all district personnel to respond to the changes.

A word of caution on the topic of positive change is in order. External experts are targeted change agents who often come in and make direct changes in a relatively short period of time. As such, there is always a risk that change processes may take unintended twists and turns. At some point, district leaders may discover that in addressing one issue or set of issues, new and/or secondary issues may emerge.

The stories in the following chapters feature external experts who have very different backgrounds, areas of expertise, approaches, skills, and services that they offer to school districts. However, each expert helped promote a shared belief in moving the district forward, facilitating growth and improvement for schools and students. They also shared other important similarities worth noting:

1. *These experts possess a national perspective that may or may not be directly related to education.* Most of the experts featured in this book work with school districts in many parts of the country, and as a result, gain a national perspective in their area of expertise. In some cases, these individuals have extensive experience outside of education, so they bring a multi-discipline perspective with them as well. These varied perspectives help experts analyze each district in relation to how other districts across the nation are faring on the same and similar issues.
2. *Working with these experts demand study, reflection, and struggle.* The experts discussed in this book do not provide easy solutions or quick fixes. Rather, they seek to deepen understanding and to suggest and develop strategies and implementations specifically tailored to the district's needs. These experts promote awareness for a variety of district stakeholders so that their work is lasting and meaningful. As noted by Weick (2009)

"... mindful organizations have struggled through periods of confused complexity on the way to their profound simplicity.... Mindless organizations ... tend to settle for the first superficial simplicity they stumble onto, and as a result know neither themselves nor their environment very well" (pp. 20–21). The experts featured in this book are exemplary for their focus on hard work to achieve profound simplicity.

3. *These experts usually create more questions than answers.* At first glance, this observation may seem like a bad thing, but a problem or issue that requires an external expert is typically not one that has easy answers. The creation of more questions as a result of the expert's work can be excellent evidence that deeper levels of the problem or issue are being uncovered and that the real work of making change is truly underway. In the end, the creation of more questions ultimately results in all stakeholders working more earnestly and effectively to find answers and to create solutions that will be real and lasting.

4. *These experts have pursued innovation by challenging the status quo.* Sometimes it is not the message alone that creates a high level of impact, but the messenger and the way the message is delivered. For example, an external expert can come in and make many of the same challenges to the status quo that perhaps a district leader has already made. However, the external expert likely has a deeper level of knowledge and experience on the subject, and he or she may be able to frame and present the challenges to the status quo in ways that district leaders cannot, often with relevant experience and research. That is, the expert can often question the status quo and present new approaches and alternatives more effectively than a district leader.

5. *These experts foster a climate for positive development and growth.* Regardless of the length of time the expert has been contracted with the district, each has effectively laid the groundwork for facilitating new development and growth. That is, these experts did not merely come in, give a presentation with the intention of getting attendees excited (or pitching a product), and leave. These external experts came in and took positive steps toward articulating the need, putting forth a customized plan, and actively creating a sustained climate for development and growth. Several of these experts developed that climate by addressing the needs of a variety of internal and external publics and creating plans that targeted a wide audience over a prolonged period of time.

As mentioned above, each expert discussed in this book brings a very different skill set, experience, and perspective to the district. Each was selected for his or her track record, reputation, and/or perceived match with the district for the particular issue or challenge addressed, and each successfully delivered what was promised. Table 1.2 a brief overview of the external experts that will be discussed in detail throughout the book.

Dr. Ray Golarz

Dr. Ray Golarz promotes a model of participatory leadership at all levels of district functioning. Participatory leadership focuses on the roles of internal audiences (primarily teachers, administrators, and board members) and the governance structure for the district. The pure participatory leadership model is almost entirely site-based. After working extensively with the principles of participatory leadership, a hybrid model was developed, combining site-based and central-office based models. This hybrid model of participatory leadership facilitates increased interaction and collaboration among district and building leaders by clarifying school and central office authority and responsibility. Understanding the interactive dynamics at play with the school board, the superintendent, principals, and teachers help facilitate a clear decision-making model.

Dr. Golarz made other significant contributions to the district. He diagnosed communication problems within the district and helped the district develop plans to address those problems. Dr. Golarz helped the district determine the level of school-based versus central office-based decision-making, and worked effectively to accommodate core value agreements and disagreements among district leaders. In the later years of his service to the district, he served as a personal advisor to the superintendent. His work helped to create a strong sense of ownership among district stakeholders, particularly among teachers who served in leadership roles and principals.

Dr. John Odom

Dr. John Odom promotes a message of inclusion and reality in his work as a diversity specialist. Dr. Odom was hired to address the achievement gap that existed in the district between minority students and white students, and to help teachers in a traditionally mostly-white community learn to better understand the implications of the changing cultural composition of the student population. Dr. Odom provided information and facilitated discussion around current cultural differences and similarities to establish a baseline to which most people in the community could relate. He combined this approach with his belief in the hope of the future, which reinforced the need for each student to grow and achieve. His message of the importance of economics (which he termed "the color green") is especially thought-provoking (Odom, 2001).

Table 1.2. Summary of External Experts

	Dr. Ray Golarz	Dr. John Odom	Mr. Wm. Strauss	Mr. Quint Studer	Mr. Ken Trump	Ms. Carol Wirth
Area of Expertise	Participatory Leadership and Decision-Making	Diversity and Student Achievement	Generational differences, student/parent characteristics	Healthcare leadership techniques in public school setting	School Safety	Financial Specialist
Time with the District	1996–2008 1–2 visits per year	2000–2008 4–5 visits per year	2005—one presentation	2007—present daily—ongoing	2008–09 4 to five times per year	1985–present weekly/monthly—ongoing
General "Lessons Learned"	• Need for understanding power of participation • Importance of decision-making variables • Importance of determining baseline core values of leaders	• Significance of economic variables • Importance of high expectations for all students	• Why knowing characteristics of Boomer, GenX, and Millenial generations matter • How to teach Millenial generation students and interact effectively with GenX parents	• Importance of assessing leadership through objective, measureable means • How techniques used in medical model can be used in education, e.g., rounding	• Specifics of new, federally approved model for crisis management • How to update, refine, and detail safety plans at the building and district levels	• Gained increased understanding of complex financial issues • Assisting district with long-range plans and decisions at critical junctures
Example of Tangible Impact (Change and/or Product)	• Decision-making process • Superintendent's Advisory Committee proposal process	• Analysis of minority student achievement data	• Specific techniques to improve staff relations, parent relations, and staff/student interactions	• Specific techniques implemented: Leadership Evaluation Measurement (LEM), rounding, Standards of Professional Behavior	• Hazard Assessments in building throughout the district • Improved emergency procedures and drills	• Effectively managed investments of funds and referendum bonds

Mr. William Strauss

Historian and author Mr. William Strauss considered leadership and growth from a global generational viewpoint. That is, Mr. Strauss stressed the importance of administrators being aware of generational differences within a common educational environment. Mr. Strauss's visit to the district was prompted by questions some administrators raised regarding the most effective ways to work with staff, parents, and students of different generations. Because each generation has different values regarding education, a new approach was necessary for reviewing communications, policies, and operations in the district.

Although Mr. Strauss only appeared in the district for one presentation, his insights had a lasting impact on the district. The distinction between Mr. Strauss's presentation and some other one-time presentations given in school districts is that Mr. Strauss was not promoting a new product, program or initiative, nor was he advocating for specific change. Rather, Mr. Strauss was engaged to deliver an informational presentation to district administrators that provided insightful and useful frameworks and tools for considering the differences among generations. This information did not require specific follow-up or action.

The success of the presentation was assessed by asking principals whether the information presented was helpful in daily interactions with staff, students, and parents of different generations. Initial reactions to this inquiry were positive, and over a year later, principals were still discussing the information that was presented and discovering new ways to make it useful in the schools.

Mr. Quint Studer

Mr. Quint Studer's work is primarily focused on leadership in health care. His work in health care places particular emphasis on the need for long-term and meaningful increases in patient satisfaction by increasing leaders' accountability and employee satisfaction and accountability. Mr. Studer's tools and techniques are very practical, and they stress administrative accountability and training for all staff, especially leaders. A variety of tools and techniques are designed to work together to align all activities to the mission, vision, and goals for an organization. When implemented properly in health care, the result of Studer's program is a dramatic culture shift, resulting in less employee turnover, more satisfied patients and employees, and reduced costs and increased business for the hospital.

Mr. Ken Trump

Mr. Ken Trump is a safety and security specialist who was hired by the district to provide a comprehensive package of services as part of the implementation for the Readiness and Emergency Management for Schools (REMS) federal grant. Those services included: (1) hazards assessments of district schools, charter schools, affiliated day care facilities, and the central office; (2) training for administrators and representatives from all areas of staffing, including teachers, aides, secretarial staff, custodial staff, and food service staff; and (3) simulation activities called "table top" exercises for Building Emergency Response Teams, liaison officers, and administrators. (Board members and local agency representatives were invited to training and table top exercises.)

In addition to the activities listed above, special training sessions were held for local media representatives, volunteers, support staff, and local private school personnel. Mr. Trump also provided a great deal of guidance about how best to implement and document the REMS grant. This guidance helped the district maximize the benefits of implementing the grant and ensured that a high level of compliance with the federal grant requirements was maintained throughout the implementation process.

Ms. Carol Wirth

Ms. Carol Wirth is a financial expert who was hired by the district on a regular basis to handle complex financial issues that required a high level of specific expertise. That is, Ms. Wirth was hired by the district primarily to help manage bond funds related to building referendums and to help the district manage post employment benefits. Both of these items required a large amount of time and specialized, detail-oriented work. Ms. Wirth worked closely with the director of business services and the district comptroller. She made presentations to the school board and superintendent to help them better understand complex district financial issues, including the bond management process, fund balance, and options for allocating funds for post employment benefits.

STAKEHOLDER INVOLVEMENT AND FUNDING

Each external expert had different levels of interactions with internal and external stakeholders in the district. It is important to know the audiences that will be affected by the external expert's presence and activities to facilitate communication about the expert and build successful relationships between the expert and those with whom he or she will be working. In addition, these different levels of interactions had a significant affect on each expert's visibility in the district. Some of the experts were highly visible and garnered media attention, while others worked more quietly behind the scenes.

An external expert is a unique member of the district team, and the district leader should be aware of the internal audiences and external publics being affected by the expert's presence.

Table 1.3 indicates the involvement level of key stakeholder groups. In addition, a summary of the sources used to fund each expert is also included.

District leaders inevitably face several challenges as change agents in moving a district forward and striving to achieve the best possible education for all students. These challenges include large-scale systems in need of change, sensitive and/or deep-seated issues that need to be addressed, and/or the need to keep new and fresh ideas, perspectives, and frameworks in the forefront to prevent stagnation and complacency. In order to effectively address all of these issues, a district leader relies on a wide variety of resources outside of the school district, both locally and outside of the community.

Resources available to a school district may be privately or publicly funded, and may or may not have a cost attached to their use. Which resources to use under which conditions is one of the many sets of questions a school leader must answer in order to determine whether the effort and expense of hiring an external expert is worth the investment and is likely to yield the desired outcomes.

Stereotypes regarding consultants have resulted in recent negative connotations about the value of their use. Interestingly, a renewed emphasis has been placed on cultivating expertise within school districts. While cultivating internal expertise has significant merit, the use of external experts in certain circumstances can move the district forward and provide a knowledgeable and fresh perspective that other models cannot.

The decision about whether or not to hire an external expert is an important one, and several questions should be considered before deciding to hire an external expert. When the decision has been made to seek the services of an external expert, it is important that the district leaders clearly articulate and define the expertise being sought. The engagement of an external expert constitutes an important relationship for everyone involved. It should be treated as a partnership, and include an appropriate match between the district and the expert.

The district leader has a responsibility to recognize his or her personal needs for professional development. In addition to facilitating positive changes for the district, an external expert can often also provides invaluable professional development to district leader as a collateral part of the change

Table 1.3. Summary of Stakeholder Involvement and Funding for External Experts

	Dr. Golarz	Dr. Odom	Mr. Strauss	Mr. Studer	Mr. Trump	Ms. Wirth
Board Involvement	High	Medium	Medium	High	Low	High
Superintendent Involvement	High	High	High	High	Medium	Medium
Director Involvement	High	High	High	High	High	High
Principal Involvement	High	High	High	High	High	Low
Teacher Leader Involvement	Medium	Low	Medium	High	Medium	Low
Parent Involvement	Low	Low	Low	Medium	Medium	Low
Funding Source	Daily Fee paid through Superintendent discretionary funds	Daily Fee paid through Superintendent discretionary funds	Daily Fee paid through Superintendent discretionary funds	Three-year donation of services valued at $1.2 million	Federal Grant	Daily Fee paid through Business Director's budget

process. Undergoing the change process is not always smooth, and working through the difficulties and challenges provides opportunities for external experts to enhance the professional development of superintendents and other stakeholders.

Ultimately, whether or not to use external experts is a decision every school leader makes. The experts in this book were chosen for their positive impact on the district, and because they represent a wide range of expert models for readers' consideration. It is hoped that the discussions in this book will familiarize readers with several contexts in which an external expert may be helpful, and will help readers recognize problems, issues, and challenges in which internal resources alone may not be sufficient to implement meaningful, lasting change.

Chapter 2

Creating Foundational System Change through Development and Adoption of a Decision-Making Model

Dr. Ray Golarz is an educational keynote speaker and expert who worked with the district over a 13-year period from 1996 to 2008. He is most noted for his pioneering work as a superintendent, implementing "site-based, shared decision-making in two different districts" (www.raygolarz.com). Dr. Golarz has provided his expertise in large districts, including Little Rock, Tulsa, and Sacramento as well as in smaller districts including Youngstown, Ohio and Riverview, Missouri. In addition, he has written several books, including his capstone work, *The Power of Participation* (Golarz & Golarz, 1995), which describes their vision for site-based management in school districts.

Dr. Golarz specific area of expertise is in helping districts develop and implement a model of decision-making tailored to their needs. This work includes measuring core values, increasing parent involvement/participation, renewing efforts to revise the teacher supervision/evaluation models, and updating the district's strategic plan. This preliminary work is followed by discussion and review to develop and implement a decision-making model. The two pure decision-making models are site based or central office/top down based; however, a mixed model may be developed that uses components from each of the pure models.

Dr. Evert first became aware of Dr. Golarz early in his first year as a superintendent. The decision to bring Dr. Golarz into the school district was the result of his appearance as a keynote speaker at the state convention for Wisconsin superintendents in the fall of 1995. Dr. Golarz was originally hired to speak to district administrators in June of 1996. Dr. Golarz's initial visit to the district was considered successful; however, the superintendent and Dr. Golarz did not appear to be well aligned in their philosophies of district leadership.

Dr. Golarz believed in a heavy emphasis on site-based management in his model of participatory leadership while Dr. Evert was initially skeptical of a model that was so heavily site based. Dr. Evert believed that a more moderate approach was necessary. It was not until after his second year as superintendent that Dr. Evert felt that he needed Dr. Golarz's input and insight about the district in order to best determine the degree of site-based management and how to facilitate this change in the district.

Dr. Evert describes how he felt and the accomplishments in the district after his first years as superintendent:

> The first two years of my superintendency were challenging. The second year was more challenging than the first year. My wife was also a new superintendent, and although I had her as a resource in addition to the other resources that were available to me, I still had several questions and doubts regarding the best direction for the district. While several important implementations were initiated during this time, I wasn't sure whether or not they would ultimately be successful. The implementations approved and initiated by the school board, administrative team, and myself in my first two years as superintendent include the following:
> - *Reorganization of the Administrative Team:* This reorganization was approved by the board of education, and involved eliminating four supervisory positions, thus streamlining the chain of command. As a result of the reorganization, principals reported to a director, who reported to the superintendent. In addition, each of the four directors became actively involved in at least one phase of curriculum. For example, the director of business services was assigned the curricular development for, and operations of, technology.
> - *Formal Development of Superintendent's Advisory Committee:* This approach was used successfully for a number of years by my predecessor. Two principal representatives, directors, and the superintendent attended these weekly meetings. Under the formal model, meetings were focused on pre-determined agenda items with specific topics of review, and typically lasted for one to one and a half hours.
> - *Director's Meetings.* The four directors met with the superintendent three Tuesdays each month. These meetings were operational, "nitty-gritty," kitchen cabinet meetings where all subjects were presented, including calendar review and other big picture items. These meetings were originally set up to address an overriding concern that central office departments did not communicate well among themselves. While these meetings did improve communication between directors and the superintendent, concerns about central office communication were still heard fourteen years later.
> - *Board Agenda Meeting.* The board agenda was set on the first Tuesday of the month. In attendance at the board agenda meeting were the directors, the

board president, two board committee chairs, the assistant board clerk, and the secretary to the superintendent.
- *Referendum.* The district developed a referendum plan to seek taxpayer approval to build a new elementary school, renovate two elementary schools, and to install a new $10-million dollar technology infrastructure throughout the district. The total cost of this referendum was over $21 million dollars. The referendum passed in February 1997 by a mere 24 votes (with over 10,000 votes cast). A recount was conducted to confirm the numbers.
- *School Visits.* When I started as superintendent, I made a commitment to visit every school every month, which I did for over 12 years. Not only did I feel that these visits were important for me, but principals told me early on that they wanted me to visit them at their school.

Despite these implementations and successes, I was restless and thought I was implementing change too slowly. I read Dr. Jerry Patterson's work, *Leadership for Tomorrow's Schools,* (1993), and he stated that the change process is slower than he had originally thought. Dr. Patterson became critical of the rapid pace of change he employed as a superintendent in a large Wisconsin district. Instead of rapid change, he was promoting a seven- to ten-year commitment for a superintendent to see real systemic change in a district. I also attended a workshop where Dr. Patterson spoke and confirmed that the pace of systemic change is a slow one.

As a result of these insights from Dr. Patterson, I slowed down. I started to breathe; however, I also started to worry in a different way. I asked myself how I could monitor the change in the district and my role in the change process. How could I assess the climate of the district? Who could I rely on for periodic, objective appraisals of my performance? Who could I count on to provide ideas for improvement based on prior knowledge and expert assessment as a result of several short visits/consultations? I thought of Ray.

Before beginning a chronology of Dr. Golarz's work with the district, it is worth taking a moment to describe the ways in which issues have changed in the school district since Dr. Golarz first worked with the district in 1997. That is, several issues that are of concern in a 2011–2012 economy and climate were not such major concerns 14 years earlier. In 1997, the major concerns of the district centered around an increasing poverty level among the student population, the need to implement technology to a higher level, and the beginning of regular and significant revenue shortfalls due to a state funding formula whose revenues did not keep pace with mandatory salary and benefit increases.

In today's educational climate, issues such as severe and regular revenue shortfalls, changes in teacher salary structures and negotiations processes, contentious relationships between the board and superintendent, and compliance with No Child Left Behind (NCLB) are major issues in the district that did not demand much attention in 1997. Several changes at the state and local levels have caused this shift in priorities, not the least of which is a slightly declining student population in the school district since about 2006, resulting in more severe and regular revenue shortfalls since that time. In addition, since 2006, the community has lost several major employers, federal and state mandates have increased, and the economy has taken a dramatic downturn. These factors have all contributed to a different educational climate today than existed in 1997.

Throughout the time that Dr. Golarz was retained by the district, the board approved a superintendent's budget for experts. This budget was used to provide professional development for staff at the discretion of the superintendent. This budget enabled the superintendent to hire keynote speakers and other resource experts in addition to covering the costs for Dr. Golarz. Over his 13-year engagement, Dr. Golarz's daily rate ranged from $1500.00 to $3,000.00 per day, and he spent an average of 5 days per year in the district.

Over the next 13 years, Dr. Golarz would have a significant impact on the superintendent and the school district as he offered valuable insight, advice, suggestions, and direction to implement change in the district. The work of Dr. Golarz is an excellent example of how an external expert can facilitate systemic change in a district over time. In order to illustrate the deep-seated and lasting changes that occurred in the district over a 13-year period, it is worthwhile to provide a detailed chronology of Dr. Golarz's work with the district. This chronology will not only illustrate the degree of change that took place, but will also illustrate the ways that the relationship between the superintendent, district, and external expert grew and evolved into something much richer and more valuable to the district than was originally intended.

THE EVOLUTION AND APPROVAL OF A PARTICIPATORY MODEL: 1997–2000

June 1997

This foundational session with Dr. Golarz was intended to provide an overview of the most pressing issues in the district and to determine appropriate direction and next steps. Several issues were discussed in this session, including: (1) improving parent involvement; (2) increasing efforts to revise the teacher supervision/evaluation model; (3) reviewing the goals for the district's first long-range strategic plan, which was formally adopted by the board of education in 1995 (titled *Beyond 2000*); and (4) clarifying expectations for principals and assistant principals for the 1997–98 school year.

While all of these items received attention, the main focus of the session was to begin the process of determining the degree to which decisions should be made at the school level, the district level, and/or the board level. This process would ultimately take nearly 3 years to complete and the resulting model continues to be used successfully over 10 years later. Dr. Golarz was instrumental in guiding the district through the assessment process and the model development. Dr. Evert recalls:

> The administrative team had been struggling with how decisions were made in our district and there were various opinions as to whether and to what extent our district should be "site based" versus when the board and/or superintendent should decide issues. This session began the process of change on perhaps our most important mission and operational issue—how to develop and come to consensus on a relevant decision-making model for the district.

Another important foundation-laying item that Dr. Golarz facilitated during his first formal session with the district was determining the administrative team members' core values in four critical dimensions or areas: Involvement/Empowerment, Risk-taking, Instructional and Curricular Flexibility, and Assessment. Using survey instruments developed by Dr. Golarz (1995), the following insights into the core values of the administrative team were revealed:

- Involvement/Empowerment: The district was viewed as "continually attempting to meaningfully involve all members of the organization and its constituencies (to a somewhat lesser degree) in decision-making" by a 3:1 margin over a less-involved approach.
- Risk-taking: The district was viewed as placing a "high value on continually exploring ways to improve at all levels and encouraging all members of the organization to try new things" by a 93 percent to 7 percent margin. However, when respondents were asked whether or not this philosophy was actually implemented, 35 percent indicated "yes, it is happening" and 65 percent indicated "no, it is not happening." In other words, although respondents seemed to feel that the climate was conducive to making improvements through trying new things, not enough action was being taken in this dimension.
- Instructional and Curricular Flexibility: Administrators held a favorable view of this dimension. Ninety-five percent of respondents indicated that the district had:

- a clear direction/mission/purpose created in part by community and district leaders;
- performed a complete analysis of "all ventures and new and old practices" of the district in terms of how they aligned to the mission of the district; and
- embraced the concept that changes could come from any level of the organization.
- Assessment: *Note: Readers are asked to keep in mind that this scale was rated at the height of the standards movement, both nationally and in Wisconsin. State standards and reporting public scores on state-wide assessments dominated conversations.* Administrators were asked about their own values and about community values. Ninety-five percent of administrators believed that the community favored traditional and/or standardized assessments, while the administrators and teachers favored alternative assessments, such as portfolios.

Based on the work done during the June 1997 sessions, Dr. Golarz made several recommendations, with an overarching focus on having the administrative team consider the best ways to empower various stakeholders. Most of the recommendations focused around the results of the core value assessments, which provided the administrative team with a framework for discussing many issues related to the four critical dimensions/areas assessed. For example, it was important to discuss and better understand the differences between the administrators' high value on alternative assessments and the ways the administrative team believed the community placed a high value on traditional assessments.

An important concept for conducting these discussions over the coming months involved establishing what Dr. Golarz called a "condition for debate." Establishing a condition for debate involved ensuring as much as possible that participants did not feel judged or threatened, and that a commonality of language existed to underpin the discussion. Dr. Golarz suggested that participants in discussions were never asked to identify their core value assessment results, although those individuals who wanted to share that information should feel free to do so. Following these guidelines and using the common terminology established in the core value assessment scales and engaging in meaningful discussion created this desirable condition for debate.

In summary, the first comprehensive visit Dr. Golarz made to the school district provided the administrative team with several tools and insights from which to build upon in future sessions. The tools included a new framework and assessment from which to consider and discuss fundamental issues around educational philosophy. The insights included the results of the core value assessments, which enabled administrators to identify and clarify ways that they and their colleagues felt about many core value issues in education.

December 1997

This session built upon the meetings of the previous June. During the intervening months, the administrative team met several times to review and to consider the implications and deeper meanings associated with the core value assessment results as well as next steps for action. Dr. Golarz met with the administrative team specifically to discuss issues related to Involvement/ Empowerment, focusing on interactions with the school board. Throughout the session, administrators identified several ways in which they were not feeling adequately supported or guided by the actions and directions of the board. administrators expressed widespread feelings of disconnect with the board. A sample of the specific items included the following:

- Some administrators felt that when the board disagreed with them on various policy and program recommendations that they were being "hung out to dry."
- Various committees would work over a period of time to conscientiously develop policy or create work product, and then the board would suddenly change it without going back to the committees when the policy or work product was presented.
- Administrators were asked to develop ideas, and when those ideas were developed, support and funding would not be approved for any level of implementation.
- A district-wide committee studied weighted grading and recommended changes to the weighted grading policy; however, the board voted 6–3 against the initiative.
- School teams studied block scheduling and recommended implementation at one of the two high schools; however, the board voted that it must be implemented in both high schools or not at all. As a result, block scheduling was not implemented in either high school.
- Administrators raised questions about the ideal level of automny (site-based management) for each school. Administrators asked how various levels of autonomy would affect the following: (1) decision-making, (2) staff development, (3) curriculum, and (4) assessment procedures.
- Administrators wanted to know how the board defined empowerment and wanted to know when the board believed that the line was crossed between empowerment and insubordination.

- Administrators wanted to discuss and formally articulate the critical attributes that gave the school district its unique identity. They also wanted to determine what level of flexibility and autonomy at the school level might be implemented without sacrificing those qualities that positively identified the district. Examples of issues that might be affected by the answers to these questions include: (1) block scheduling, (2) full-day kindergarten, (3) school uniforms, (4) school choice, and (5) naming a new elementary school.

An important component of this session was getting the board actively involved in the process, so that board members and administrators would begin to understand one another and come to a general consensus about the underlying framework under which they would operate. Seven of nine board members were in attendance during these sessions, and they took the same core values assessments that were taken by administrators during the first session earlier in the year. The survey results of board members revealed the following:

- *Involvement/Empowerment:* The board was close to evenly split regarding whether or not all district staff should have a say in decision-making or whether board members should get input before decisions are made.
- *Risk-taking:* Eighty-six percent of the board believed strongly in encouraging risk-taking among administrators.
- *Instructional Strategy and Curricular Flexibility:* All board members taking the core values assessments believed that curricular changes could be initiated by anyone in the district; and moreover, should be.
- *Assessment:* The board was close to evenly split regarding whether traditional and/or standardized assessments were preferable to alternative assessments.

After reviewing the results of the core values assessments taken by board members, Dr. Golarz analyzed the information and asked board members the following questions based on the assessment results:

- Would you as a board be willing to support fundamental architectural differences in individual schools if the respective school community is in support of these differences? For example, if parents and staff wanted a non-graded school at the elementary level, would the board support it?
- How comfortable are you as a board in terms of empowering administrative staff with overall decision making? For example, is it necessary for the board to see a complete list of all capital equipment in the budget, or would it be sufficient for the board to receive an overview of the prioritization process for capital equipment items?

- Would you as a board be willing to support a more aggressive minority hiring quota?
- Are you as a board willing to allow one or more schools to be wholly site based in terms of management and decision making?

These questions were designed to help board members clarify their own framework for decision making, so that requests for policy development and work product creation were in better alignment with values and action steps that the board would be likely to support. Another goal of the discussion was to provide administrators and teachers with better guidance and direction for future actions through open dialogue, which was facilitated by honest answers to the questions above. That is, administrators would have a much better idea about what the board would likely support and why they would support it. In addition, the answers to these questions would help to clarify areas where the administration and board were polarized, and perhaps foster further discussion about the reasons for polarization and whether there were any actions that could be taken that could help increase the level of alignment between the two groups.

During this session, Dr. Golarz also met with the board and the administrative team to begin discussion about strategies that could be used to improve the alignment between the two groups. In order to direct these discussions, Dr. Golarz posed several questions for both groups to consider over the course of the upcoming months:

- Is the goal of the organization to move to a certain point on each of the four core value dimensions/areas (Involvement/Empowerment, Risk Taking, Instructional Strategy and Curricular Flexibility, and Assessment)?
- Is it the goal of the organization that everyone be closer together on each of the core value dimensions/areas?
- Is the board willing to take risks, such as allowing block scheduling in one high school?
- Is the administrative bureaucracy standing in the way of really addressing problems?
- Is the board continuing to study and approve initiatives that are already in place in some form (financially and politically) and neglecting some new initiatives that need board support for their success?

This session helped the administration determine to what level the board would support increased empowerment of administration and staff, and to what degree they might support a model of participatory leadership. It is interesting to note that when the process began with Dr. Golarz nearly a year and a half earlier, it began with a superintendent who was interested in figuring out how to address more difficult, long-term problems in the district. Addressing the long-term problems involved assessing leadership groups on two different sides of the educational leadership equation: administrators and board members. Dr. Golarz's assessments enabled members from both groups to acknowledge and better understand their own core values and to determine where those core values were aligned and where they were between and within both groups.

During the course of these visits, the superintendent received valuable, although general information about administrators and board members through a limited amount of private counsel from Dr. Golarz regarding the management of those leadership groups. It is important to note that Dr. Golarz, as with any good expert, was always very aware that some of the interactions he was facilitating were very sensitive in nature. Although the superintendent and Dr. Golarz did not always agree, the meetings between the two were always civil and marked by a tone of mutual concern and respect.

At no time during meetings with the superintendent would Dr. Golarz reference any particular individual or pass along any specific comments. That course of action would simply have been counterproductive. It was in the best interest of all to have sensitive positive and negative comments objectively delivered to the superintendent by an external professional expert. Dr. Golarz had a strong commitment to engaging in difficult work with civility and trust, and modeled that civility and trust throughout his years in the district.

June, September, November 1998

The June 1998 visit consisted of an in-depth analysis of the work completed by the board, superintendent, directors, and administrative team over the previous six months. Dr. Golarz presented a summary regarding the efforts of the board and administrators to consider increased administrative empowerment with a greater focus on shared governance. The board and administrators had discussed ramifications of changing the decision-making model on the empowerment level of administrators, and the possible consequences that might predictably result from such a change. An important part of this discussion was the acknowledgement that the core values of the board (as identified in Dr. Golarz's core value assessment) were closely aligned with the core values of the administration; however, both sides understood that a change of board membership could alter this alignment.

The September 1998 meetings with Dr. Golarz resulted in significant steps being taken toward adopting a formal model of participatory leadership within the district. Dr. Golarz's meetings with administrators and the district's manager of public information focused on the next steps needed to move the district forward in the participatory form of educational governance. Because the district had an informal decision-making model committee in place before the work with Dr. Golarz formally began, and it was agreed that this committee work would continue to operate in the new model because it was aligned with the new emphasis the board, superintendent, and administration were placing on participatory leadership. Throughout the process of working toward formal adoption of the new decision-making model, participatory leadership was evolving as the customary, accepted term used to describe and pursue the district's work with Dr. Golarz.

During this session, the work with the board also focused on issues related to the ongoing development of participatory leadership and the district's decision-making model, most notably how the division of decision making should be allocated between the central office, the schools, and the board. Placing site-based and central-office based decision making models on a continuum, Dr. Golarz stated his belief that the district should not adopt a decision making model at either extreme end of the continuum based on his analysis of the district, including leadership groups and teachers. That is, the district should not be a district of schools where each school is in charge of what is taught and how it is taught. Nor did he advocate that the board and the superintendent alone determine what is taught and how it is taught. Instead, Dr. Golarz suggested that a more appropriate model would consist of having the board determine the "what" of instructional focus, and allowing the administration and schools to determine the "how" to achieve the instructional focus.

Dr. Golarz was able to offer the board specific guidance during this session regarding strategies for determining the "what" of instructional focus. He also included guiding parameters on board authority, so that the board could establish some boundaries for itself that would make it function more effectively with administrators, staff, and parents to better serve the student population. This guidance included the following suggestions and ideas:

- Board members should remember that latitude and authority does not mean exclusive authority.
- Parent involvement must be tied to specific issues and parameters.
- Consider how each school's Continuous Growth Plan will be affected by the board's "what" decisions.
- Consider how new plans or proposals would be supported by teachers and parents.
- Gather, review, and consider research findings and other data on new ideas before deciding to adopt them.
- Have an evaluation and/or assessment plan in place to determine the effectiveness of a new plan or proposal.

- Discuss and consider how a plan or proposal would affect higher or lower grade levels and schools not involved in the plan or proposal.
- Consider the fiscal implications of any new plan or idea, and consider issues of fiscal neutrality when considering the "what" for any specific grade or school.
- Discuss and consider whether the plan or proposal is morally, legally, and ethically correct and in the best interest of student learning.

The pace of the change process was moving steadily, but seemed slow due to the intermittent nature of Dr. Golarz's visits and the fact that tangible results seemed near at hand, but were not yet reality. As a result, Dr. Golarz suggested several practical procedures and protocols that could help make the transition to and implementation of the new decision making model successful. He stressed the importance of meeting regularly to continue moving the process forward by clearly identifying next steps for action. It was also important to assign responsibilities and assess progress through regular reporting to ensure action steps were being implemented and completed. During all phases of the implementation process and beyond, it was critical to keep accurate records. All of these practical suggestions helped leadership groups track the progress of the initiative.

Most of the suggestions above were intended to address problems associated with the effects of long-established sets of policies and practices in the district. These habits were affecting the commitment to, and successful implementation of, the new participatory leadership model. Dr. Golarz observed that the district had functioned for a very long time under a particular way of doing business that no longer reflected the new emerging philosophy. He believed that perhaps this misalignment was hindering forward momentum, and that it was time to consider reviewing policies and practices so that they accurately reflected the new philosophy. Changing several policies and practices enabled the district moved forward more effectively with the participatory leadership model.

Dr. Golarz pointed out that principals and other administrative team members are not adversarial by nature. Individuals in these administrative categories will not generally object to new ideas for the sake of objection. However, during this time of change, there were two distinct attitudes represented in the administrative team, which created adversarial tension at times. One group was ready for new and increased levels of participation and they were excited about having a greater voice in the decision-making process.

The other group was not ready for the change. These individuals did not want to be disagreeable or go to war over the changes in the decision-making model; they were simply satisfied with the status quo. It was important to address this administrative misalignment, because the misalignment prevented positive progress. The administrative team needed to come to resolution and become a cohesive group to move the entire district forward in a meaningful manner that would result in improved educational opportunities for students.

Dr. Golarz identified a likely reason for the resistance demonstrated by some administrative team members. The old model was a shared information model and the new model would be a shared decision-making model, and this important distinction created the resistance. Administrators under the old model did not have the formal authority to make many of their own decisions at the building level, and as such, administrators uncomfortable with risk taking were able to successfully maintain the status quo. The security of receiving direction from the central office was very comforting to these administrators, and they were understandably uncomfortable and hesitant about engaging in a participatory decision-making model.

On the other end of the spectrum, some building administrators wanted more input in decision-making at the building level than was appropriate for the district's emerging model of participatory leadership. These building administrators wanted to be the primary decision-makers at their buildings, following a purely site-based model. They believed that they knew the needs of their students and staff better than the central office. These administrators had ideas for improving their buildings and the staff support to implement those ideas.

Dr. Golarz believed it was important for senior-level administrators, beginning with the superintendent, to engage in the new model first. The superintendent's immediate challenge was to bring both sides toward the middle. Dr. Golarz made several specific suggestions to help the superintendent unify the direction of the administrative team:

- Discuss continued adherence to old policies and procedures that reflect the old model to discover what is preventing stakeholders from participating in the new model.
- Model support for the new initiative starting at the central office. The superintendent and directors should strive to increase administrative support for the new model from a current perceived level of 25 percent to 75 percent.
- Clarify the rules of engagement in the decision-making model. Administrators must understand that even with a customized participatory model, there are some decisions that one person (typically the superintendent) must and should make.

- Remain sensitive to the fact that some of the old practices are held near and dear to certain administrators. There is an ongoing need to be sensitive to change processes that will create undue conflict.
- Communicate timelines and make certain administrators understand what items are under district control and what items are under the control of the state-level Department of Instruction (DPI). Most principals do not fully understand how central office operates; that is, central office can move much more quickly than principals think. The central office has an image of being a slow mover, which simply is not true.
- Consider how to assess the effectiveness of the change in models among administrators.

1997 and 1998 were important years in moving forward with the participatory model of decision-making. The critical importance of leadership becoming aware and knowledgeable about the school district became very evident at this time. That is, it is extremely difficult to become the organization leaders envision if they do not know intimately and in detail the organization they currently *are*. This journey toward a new model of decision-making and leadership was as much a journey of discovering and defining what the district was so that purposeful, meaningful steps could be taken toward making lasting change.

This process would have been arguably impossible without the perspective and guidance of a knowledgeable and perceptive external expert. Dr. Golarz provided a fresh perspective that those who were enmeshed in the organization could not. Dr. Golarz also provided a wealth of experience on the subject of site-based management and had seen various configurations of participatory leadership work in many other districts. As Dr. Evert remembers:

> Many of the things Dr. Golarz identified seemed obvious after he discussed them; however, as the superintendent, I would not necessarily have given specific identification to the observations he made (although I was aware they were present), nor would I have known how to consciously manage all of the identifications to best facilitate the participatory leadership implementation. Having Dr. Golarz's knowledge and experience provided valuable insights that not only helped the implementation of participatory leadership, but also helped me in many other aspects of my role.

November 1998–May 2000

Dr. Golarz made another visit to the district at the end of 1998 to follow up on the work done the previous two years. The core value assessments were administered again to three groups of respondents: (1) board members,

(2) principals, and (3) central office administrators. When the assessments were administered this time, respondents rated each item twice, once to indicate their own response to each item and once to indicate what they believed the district (or community) composite result would be.

Although the sample size of board members and central office respondents was smaller than expected, the results were still very telling. Each of the three groups (board, principals, central office administrators) supported a greater degree of participation in decision-making; however, they viewed the district or community as being less supportive of a participatory approach on each of the four core value assessment dimensions/areas (Empowerment, Risk-Taking, Curricular and Instructional Flexibility, and Assessment). Dr. Evert recalls:

> Most individuals, regardless of role, espoused a belief that we should get going on participatory leadership but believed that the district or community held a view that said, "Let's not move forward." This outcome was frustrating to me, because I believed individuals within the three groups collectively comprised the leadership of the district that they were rating. Did this outcome mean we had an ownership issue?

Work continued throughout 1999 and early 2000 preparing the policy proposal for the district approval process and a final board vote. Dr. Golarz recommended that the district include several independent ongoing improvement efforts to this policy proposal in order to better align all of the district's initiatives and work. These ongoing improvement efforts included the revision of a formal district long-range plan and the consideration of how to implement state academic standards. In addition, the participatory leadership model required the submission of a specific rubric to determine under what conditions ideas for change would be approved. Such ideas would be reviewed by using a formal decision-making proposal process that included consideration of the following questions:

- What research supports the proposal?
- What tools will be used to evaluate the implementation?
- Have the effects of the proposal on other schools and grade levels been discussed among building leaders?
- How does the proposal address fiscal neutrality?
- Is the proposal legally, morally, and ethically correct?
- Is there support for the proposal from district constituencies?
- What maintenance of effort will be required to properly follow through on the proposal?

The Superintendent's Advisory Committee (SAC) was a mechanism already in place under the previous superintendent to discuss issues of interest among senior leadership. This group consisted of two principal representatives, the directors, and the superintendent. Under the previous superintendent, these meetings were informal and did not require an agenda or minutes.

Under the current superintendent (before formal adoption of the participatory leadership model), the function of this group was similar but more formal. Agendas were provided and minutes of these meetings were taken and distributed to internal audiences. After the formal adoption of the participatory leadership model, all proposals for new ideas were presented to the SAC committee before any other action was taken. The minutes of these meetings were distributed to internal audiences and the local media, ensuring that all proposals received a procedurally consistent hearing. The participatory leadership model of decision-making, including the SAC proposal process, was formally approved by the board on May 9, 2000 by a 9–0 vote.

DEVELOPING AND IMPLEMENTING A PUBLIC ENGAGEMENT COMPONENT TO THE PARTICIPATORY LEADERSHIP MODEL: 2000–2009

Dr. Golarz continued to visit the district once or twice a year between 2000 and 2009 to facilitate the implementation of the participatory model of decision-making once it had been approved by the board. As a result of the participatory model, many principals had more control over their schools' professional development programs. Teachers and other staff throughout the district were encouraged to submit proposals for change through the new formal process. The process of developing, refining, approving, and implementing a customized participatory leadership model changed the climate and culture of the district.

The implementation of any new initiative is not without problems and issues, and implementing a participatory leadership model was no different. The processes suggested by Dr. Golarz worked very well in some contexts, but not so well in others, and needed adaptation in order to be effective. Specifically, the decision-making model worked well for new programs and implementations, but needed additional components to effectively manage existing and/or recurring long-term issues and problems.

Change is not necessarily a linear process, and any change being implemented occurs in established and often complex contexts. In these established contexts, there are usually some things going well and other things that are problematic. The district had significant problems with several issues that were ongoing and appeared to have no avenue toward resolution. There was no formal mechanism in place to facilitate public input on these issues; as a result, citizens were left with a small number of options to express their opinions, such as the citizen comment time during board meetings, letters to the editor, and calling or writing board members or the superintendent.

In this section, we will examine the specific problem of public engagement that arose and was addressed as part of the overall implementation of the participatory leadership model. The inclusion of a public engagement component to the participatory leadership model resulted in improved communication in both directions between the district and the community. That is, the district communicated problems and possible solutions with more frequency, transparency, and clarity to community members, and community members were given more opportunities to communicate their views to the board and administration.

Specific Issues That Required Public Engagement

Several specific issues in the district created the need to develop a public engagement model. Some of these issues were recurring and would continue to crop up year after year even when they were addressed. Other issues had reached a stalemate between leadership groups and/or the community where forward progress seemed unlikely.

One major problem with these types of issues is that the district lacked a process for appropriately channeling the public turmoil and energy generated by various controversies. As a result, individuals and groups would demonstrate their support or displeasure on issues in a variety of ways, including speaking at board meetings, calling board members and staff off the record, circulating petitions, letter writing campaigns, and writing letters to the editor. The amount of controversy, with both internal audiences and external publics, prevented a degree of consensus required to take next steps.

Many of these challenging issues were critical pieces aligned with the district's long-range plan and could be shown by research to be educationally sound. As such, it was important to engage the public to determine whether these issues should move forward, be modified in some manner, or be abandoned altogether. In short, these issues needed resolution. Examples of politically charged and/or recurring issues that drove the development of the public engagement model are described below:

- *The instruction of string instruments at the elementary school level*—String instrument instruction was provided to students in the district in grades 4 and 5. An administrative proposal was submitted that would "eliminate 4th grade

strings and develop a proposal to enhance string instruction" (board minutes, March 11, 2002). This proposal was submitted for several reasons:
- Elementary principals expressed concern that the 4th grade string program was disruptive to the overall academic program. They did not want students pulled out of reading and math class, after which students would have to make up the time. This concern was particularly important to principals because of the high-demand state tests administered in the 4th grade.
- The retention rate for string enrollment from the 4th grade to the 5th grade was less than 50 percent, which led principals to further question the value of the program as it was structured.
- The string instructors were very effective in communicating with parents, and when a change in the structure of the string program was first proposed, these teachers immediately garnered support for the existing program from parents. These parents vocally supported the existing program without understanding the reasons for, and implications of, the proposed program changes.
- Administrators wanted a high-quality string program at the elementary level, and believed that perhaps changing the structure of the program could maintain the quality of the program and address issues with students missing excessive instructional time. However, the parent and public involvement early on in the change process necessitated a higher degree of communication with the public regarding these structural changes than was currently available in the district's decision-making model.
- *Weighted Grading*—The issue of weighted grading revolved around the critical question of whether certain advanced high school classes should be worth additional honor or class rank points for graduation. By 2002, the district had approved and used weighted grading for over 20 years. There were very strong opinions on both sides of the issue from teachers, parents, and board members about whether or not the weighted grading system should be continued or whether the system should be changed to reflect a 4.0 grading system. The arguments for keeping the weighted grading system included the following:
  - Teachers and parents involved in Advanced Placement (AP) courses strongly supported the awarding of additional honors points for those classes. These teachers and parents argued that students in these classes did more work and worked at a higher academic level than students in other classes, and therefore should be recognized for their efforts.
  - Teachers and parents supporting weighted grading believed that a college transcript reflecting these honors points, and resulting in a grade point average higher than 4.0 communicated strong scholarship to colleges and universities.

- Both high schools in the district had large graduating classes, often 400 students or more. Teachers and administrators felt that there was a need to differentiate those students achieving at the highest levels to prevent a large number of valedictorians and salutatorians.

On the other side of the issue, several teachers and parents who supported a 4.0 grading scale also put forth valid arguments, including the following:

- All course work had equal merit to the students and staff involved, and if some of the regular classes needed to be made more rigorous, then they should be made more rigorous.
- One board member checked with numerous colleges and universities and found that weighted grades did not factor into consideration for admission to any significant degree.
- Parents and teachers felt that the overriding issue was equity and fairness, and that the current system established an elitist educational culture.

A board vote was taken in spring of 1997, which took place at an emotionally charged board meeting with a 6–3 vote in favor of continuing weighted grading. The issue resurfaced again five years later and the outcome was reversed when the board voted 6–3 to replace weighted grading with a 4.0 grading system. The new grading system was implemented over a four-year period.

These issues highlighted the need for a process to facilitate two-way communication between the board/administration and the community. The board and administration felt that continued input from the public through a formal public engagement process was essential to reaching decisions that reflected the needs and values of the community.

Birth of the Public Engagement Model

The participatory model of decision making described in Part I worked particularly well for new issues. Using the process, a new issue would generate a proposal to the Superintendent's Advisory Committee (SAC), which would either be approved or rejected by the committee. If approved, the proposal would continue forward according to the direction determined at the committee meeting. As mentioned in Part I, the SAC meeting minutes were recorded, including the outcomes and actions required on each proposal. These minutes were distributed throughout the district and to the local media for review.

The tangible benefits of having initiatives go through the SAC were threefold. First, the process provided a fair and accessible process that gave everyone an opportunity to have their activities and initiatives reviewed by leadership. Multiple stakeholders had access to the proposal process and could be part of the decision-making efforts. Lachman and Wlodarczyk (2011), define multiple stakeholders as internal (including teachers, staff, unions, and parents) and external (including residents, agencies, faith communities, government, and businesses).

Second, the process ensured that all activities and initiatives needing formal approval were aligned with the district's vision and mission. The approval process required the requestor to articulate the educational goals of the activity or initiative and describe the ways that it aligned to the short- and/or long-term goals in the district's strategic plan. As a result, approved requests aligned well with the district's mission and vision, and both leaders and requesters could articulate that alignment to internal audiences and external publics.

Finally, this process streamlined the workload for the board. The SAC determined which proposals needed board approval so that the board did not have to review a large number of proposals unnecessarily. By the time a proposal reached the board, members knew that the proposal met the minimum standards for supporting the educational goals and vision/mission of the district. As a result, they could focus on issues such as funding and community support for a given proposal. This process solidified the roles of each of the three leadership entities in the district (board, superintendent, principals).

However, as well as this process worked for the most part, an unanticipated problem occurred. As the process unfolded, it became apparent that not all major issues in the district were new topics that could be addressed using the SAC process. Rather, these issues (most of which could be safely described as hot-button) could be categorized as recurring or existing. Leadership described these issues as unsolvable or irresolvable. Many of these issues would continue to resurface every four to eight years.[1] Moving these existing/recurring issues forward required a different or modified decision making approach and increased opportunities for community input.

One important modification to the SAC process that was implemented to improve community involvement was opportunity for public comment, which eventually became known as public engagement. Discussion with Dr. Golarz and central office staff revealed that there was a need establish an open channel of communication with the public to address recurring, existing, and hot-button issues. Providing a structured process for involving the public to a high degree when addressing certain district issues improved the relationship between the district and the community. In addition, it improved the district climate overall. Internal audiences' comfort level with these difficult issues was increased, regardless of whether they were directly or indirectly involved with a particular issue.

Dr. Golarz was instrumental in helping create a process to facilitate public engagement. During a special board meeting on March 11, 2002. the manager of public information (MPI) and the superintendent presented the public engagement model that was developed to increase community involvement in developing solutions for certain controversial issues. A draft of the proposal is provided in Textbox 2.1:

Box 2.1 Proposed Public Engagement Process

There was a need to develop a process to address recurring and/or politically charged major issues, such as district boundary lines, grading systems, 4th grade strings, crisis communications, and referendums. The proposed process consisted of the following steps that enabled public individuals and groups to work within the district system to express their opinions and communicate ideas.

Dr. Golarz, the superintendent, and administrative team worked with the MPI on the initial proposal for a public engagement process. The material below is the initial draft of the proposed public engagement process the MPI presented to the board on March 11, 2002:

- Director consults on proposals for major changes in curriculum, program, board policy, etc. with MPI to assess possible PR issues.
- MPI reviews this model and new proposal regarding the change and meets with the director(s) and superintendent to discuss the adaptation of this action model.
- Timelines for initiating the change are developed with superintendent, directors, and MPI. Timeline will include some or all of the following:
  - Development of list of benefits and possible staff/citizen concerns with the change.
  - Written overview statement and question/answer talking points are developed from benefits/concerns list.
  - This material is organized into an explanatory white paper communication.
  - Brief video is developed using white paper information and question/answer format.
  - Convening a Citizen Advisory Committee is considered to review these points and provide feedback to white paper and video as a sample focus group for reactions and input.
  - Staff receives white paper communication prior to distribution of information to community.

- Parents receive white paper information in mailed letter and/or parent newsletter with information about upcoming community forum.
- Citizens Advisory Committee is formed (optional).
- Media is contacted with news release written from white paper information and information on the upcoming forum and advisory committee, if formed.
- Community Forum is held with members of committee in attendance (if applicable).
- Citizens Advisory Committee provides their recommendations.
- Changes are made as needed to proposal.
- Board, staff, and advisory committee receive the changed proposal or approved current proposal.
- News release is developed regarding final proposal.
- Staff and advisory committee receive news release via e-mail.
- Board hears revised proposal as presentation. Proposal reaches media as communicated at board meeting and through news release distributed evening of board meeting.
- If board is seeking to approve, proposal is scheduled for first and second readings.
- Following second reading, board updates newsletter reports on the issue. Media covering board meetings reports on the issue.

Dr. Golarz was in attendance at the special board meeting where the public engagement model was discussed. In a follow-up memo, Dr. Golarz praised the new decision-making model as appearing "extremely well constructed and coherent, providing appropriate guidance to those using the document" (Golarz, March 15, 2002) However, he also acknowledged the shortcomings of the model, stating that school leaders "represent only a portion of stakeholders who . . . [need] to support . . . [proposals] in a school district intent on moving to new levels of [stakeholder] involvement." Dr. Golarz indicated that teacher and parent support was an important component of a new proposal.

After several months of development and refinement, the board voted unanimously to approve the new public engagement process in May of 2002. While this process was initially developed to address high levels of public tension on certain politically changed issues, the public engagement process had several other positive benefits for internal audiences and external publics. Stakeholders at all levels could use the public engagement process to express opinions about existing proposals, and to suggest ideas and solutions for existing proposals and ideas for new ones. Use of the public engagement process was considered as part of every SAC proposal thereafter, regardless of

> **Box 2.2 The Public Engagement Process and Dr. Golarz's Recommendations for Budgeting**
>
> Dr. Evert recalls:
> Adding the public engagement process to the decision making model was particularly helpful in the area of budgeting in the mid-2000s. During this time, the student enrollment in the district was undergoing a small annual decline, which resulted in several years where the costs of keeping current staffing and programs outpaced the incoming revenue. Using the public engagement model, particularly regarding proposed program and staffing cuts, helped the board and administration determine the public's values and helped ensure that budget-cutting priorities aligned with public priorities.
>
> Dr. Golarz also provided several strategies and ideas that helped the district's decision-making process during difficult budgeting periods. His suggestions were designed to address the biggest causes of stress during the spring of the school year so that preparations for the following school year could proceed smoothly. Even though the suggestions seemed simple and sensible, they were challenging to implement, and they did result in a smoother process. These suggestions included: (1) starting the budgeting process early (January/February), (2) making the superintendent the point person in presenting the budget cuts, (3) using a system of equity in making the cuts, (4) employing an actuarial firm to review potential reductions and analyze long-term costs and savings, and (5) keeping the overall time frame for budget reductions as short as possible.

whether the proposal addressed a new or existing issue. The proposed public engagement process is presented in Textbox 2.2.

THE CHANGING ROLE OF THE EXTERNAL EXPERT: 2002–2008

Dr. Golarz continued to work with the district as the participatory model took root in the district and grew to become the cultural norm. As the participatory model was implemented systemically, Dr. Golarz shared his experience and knowledge and provided the district with a wealth of new information and best practices. In addition, he continued to provide the superintendent with his unique perspective regarding stakeholders' perceptions on a variety of issues. That is, he served as a sounding board to the superintendent on key issues. Dr. Evert states:

> The observations and comments that Dr. Golarz shared with me during his work with the district provided a comprehensive and in-depth view of issues

facing superintendents across the nation. In addition, his reflections and observations were uniquely tailor-made for the district as well as having broader generalizations to other districts. This broader interpretation helped me in my one-year role as president of the state superintendent's association as well as enhancing my reading of professional journals and books related to the superintendency. Throughout his time with the district, I believe I grew in my ability to think from a systems perspective while applying specific individual lessons learned to district-wide issues. Also importantly, the lessons developed from my time with Dr. Golarz greatly contributed to a very positive working environment between board and superintendent.

During the period between 2002 and 2008, the participatory leadership model was working well in the district. As a result of his excellent work and knowledge of district issues and dynamics, Dr. Golarz's role expanded and evolved to include advising the superintendent on a wide variety of culture and climate issues. He continued to visit up to two times a year, and provided opportunities for growth to the superintendent that the board and other internal resources could not be expected to provide. Dr. Golarz's insights and knowledge of the district gave him a unique perspective that was very helpful to the superintendent.

Dr. Golarz's role as advisor to the superintendent was an important one in which either person could initiate dialogue on topics of interest to the district. Sometimes, Dr. Golarz's comments reflected his observations during his visits to the districts. Other times, the superintendent identified issues and topics on which he wanted Dr. Golarz to advise him. For example, in May, 2002, the superintendent identified several items for Dr. Golarz to consider, including: (1) how best to address union leaders and staff on the issue of increasing involvement and participation at the teacher and staff levels; (2) a review of the year's budget reduction process in preparation for planning the following year's budget; (3) how to evaluate program effectiveness to determine what and when to add and subtract programs; and (4) a review of the Superintendent's Advisory Committee to determine what was working and what was not.

Dr. Golarz's advice helped the superintendent frame the issues in different ways and make subtle shifts in direction when necessary. Typically, the superintendent was not asking Dr. Golarz to help create a new course of action; rather, he was asking Dr. Golarz to help him identify times and places for "course correction." These subtle adjustments helped the superintendent move the district forward in a way that worked for internal audiences and external publics.

During the time that Dr. Golarz served the school district, the board was supportive of his involvement and with his expanded capacity as advisor to the superintendent. They considered his fees an investment in leadership.

Throughout Dr. Golarz's time of service, various board members would acknowledge that one of his primary roles was to help the superintendent. As one former board president said to the superintendent in the 2002, "Remember, Dr. Golarz is here for you, not for the board. We're paying Dr. Golarz to come in and help you with direction, challenges, confirmation, systems analysis, and your own personal planning for the district, ranging from curriculum issues to budget issues to personnel issues to board/superintendent relations."

The board's understanding of Dr. Golarz's role in the district remained consistent for several years and contributed to effective board-superintendent relationships during that time. Although board members had questioned Dr. Golarz's role in the past, the superintendent was able to engage in discussion and provide evidence and examples to board members so that they had a high comfort level regarding Dr. Golarz's value to the district.

By 2007, however, changes in board membership resulted in different understandings and a less-than-unanimous view of his role. That is, some board members viewed Dr. Golarz's role as consultant to the superintendent, some board members believed he should assist the board more directly, and yet other board members were unclear about why Dr. Golarz was hired. Ms. Van Deuren recalls a visit from Dr. Golarz shortly after she was elected to the board:

> I was very concerned about the way our board was interacting with one another. I thought Dr. Golarz was going to come in and help our board address some of these issues so that we would function as a more cohesive unit, one that could disagree respectfully on an issue, take a vote, and then support that vote. I was excited about our board workshop with Dr. Golarz, but initially came away skeptical and disappointed, because I was not clear about why he was there and what he was trying to accomplish. As I later understood, Dr. Golarz was hired largely to provide a different perspective to the superintendent, and I came to recognize that his service to the district was very valuable. In hindsight, I also recognized that, while Dr. Golarz did not address our board issues the way I would have liked at the time, he did facilitate conversation among the board that let me know that I wasn't the only board member that had concerns about the way we were conducting board business.

One and a half years later, Dr. Golarz also observed a new anxiety among administrators, teachers, and the community regarding the board. In a memo to the superintendent (November 25, 2008) Golarz states, "I was continually advised that the anxiety was emanating specifically from participation in or observation of public school board meetings." This new atmosphere was "eroding trust throughout the organization." Dr. Golarz also noted that he was hearing the same personal observations "from virtually everyone."

At the time of the memo, the superintendent had already announced his retirement, and Dr. Golarz noted that such an atmosphere of eroded trust could negatively affect the quality and number of candidates that might apply for the superintendent's position. As it happened, the number of applications for the superintendent's position was significantly lower than it had been in previous searches. Whether or not the reduced candidate pool was the result of eroded trust is arguable; however, Dr. Golarz's experience-based caution was realized.

Reflecting back on the later years that Dr. Golarz worked with the district, it appears that a combination of three factors worked together to create a different climate and culture in the district than existed in the early 2000s: (1) a change in the board's collective priorities and attitudes, (2) a new initiative with a health care leadership model and expert, and (3) the superintendent's imminent retirement. As a result of these three factors, Dr. Golarz's role was diminished in 2007–2008, and his final session with the district was in November of 2008.

The role of the superintendent is service-oriented. As such, it is all too easy for the superintendent to act as a sounding board for everyone else, while overlooking his or her own needs for such a sounding board. While that sounding board may be a spouse, another superintendent, or a close, long-time friend, having an external expert act as that sounding board can alleviate the need to have someone with whom to talk, and can result in improved planning for direction in the district. Dr. Golarz was in a unique position to act as that sounding board for the superintendent during the latter part of his tenure in the district. He had the advantage of being an outsider with a neutral and unbiased perspective, yet his extensive work with the district over many years provided him with knowledge of the climate and cultural nuances that existed therein.

LESSONS LEARNED

Because Dr. Golarz worked regularly with the district over a long period of time, he observed long-term growth and change in the district. In June, 2008, Dr. Golarz stated the following:

> The culture of the ... [district] schools is so healthy that no one even noticed the fact that the heads of all these organized groups [union, board, administration] were comfortable together in the office of the superintendent with a consultant and board president and no agenda limitations. The meeting was cordial, filled with occasional and appropriate laughter, and a strong sense of openness.

Late in the superintendent's tenure, Dr. Golarz made several other observations on the positive aspects of the school climate, including focus on student achievement and learning, balance in hiring internal and external administrators, and ample opportunity to discuss a wide range of issues in a civil manner among stakeholders. These positive aspects of the district were observed even as the free and reduced lunch rate (an indicator of poverty in the district) tripled in ten years, and the district staff and board were able to address the impacts of these economic changes.

The extended process of developing and implementing the participatory leadership model in the district created a foundation upon which effective and efficient school governance operated for over a decade. As Dr. Golarz stated in a letter sent to the superintendent in November of 2008:

> The district's participatory model is now in the early stages of its second decade of success. When initiated, no one could really predict its evolution, for its implementation was in the hands of multiple groups including the school board, administrative team, teachers, and various community members. As it has evolved it has fostered a set of organized habits that have now spread to all corners of the organization.

The work and experiences with Dr. Golarz generated a number of tangible benefits for the district and positively impacted the district's leadership groups (board, superintendent, administrative team). Because Dr. Golarz's work with the district spanned such a long period of time, the participatory leadership model was allowed to fully evolve and mature under his guidance. As a result, it is possible to consider the entire process and to extrapolate several lessons learned that may be useful to other superintendents and district leaders.

Perhaps the most obvious lesson learned is that there are indeed times when a district leader needs the help of an external expert to provide an unbiased perspective and to act as a sounding board. Dr. Golarz served as a highly regarded advisor and provided objective opinions regarding the needs and conditions of the district. The new superintendent appreciated the unbiased perspective Dr. Golarz brought when he began work in the district. The same superintendent, with more experience in later years, valued the longitudinal knowledge of the district and Dr. Golarz's national perspective. During the entire span of Dr. Golarz's time with the district his observations, opinions, advice, and knowledge were valuable to the board, superintendent, and administrative team, which in turn served to positively impact the district and the community.

A second lesson learned working with Dr. Golarz was the importance of maintaining a cohesive, aligned direction during the implementation process of a new major initiative. Implementing a model of participatory leadership in the district was much like rebuilding the foundation of a house. The work of change in the decision-making model required all of the district leadership groups to rethink and reevaluate the vision, mission, and short- and long-term goals for the district.

Maintaining a cohesive, aligned direction for progress was made even more challenging because various initiatives to improve student learning and achievement were underway at the same time. Dr. Golarz was able to assist district efforts to align various initiatives by becoming involved with long-range planning efforts, developing a formal decision-making model, and guiding the logistics of various other initiatives.

As often occurs when a major initiative is underway, the inevitable process of adaptation moves the implementation in different directions than perhaps was originally intended. While this adaptation is arguably necessary, there is a point at which the integrity and intention of the model may be compromised. Dr. Golarz's continued guidance throughout the process ensured that the district's adaptations of the participatory leadership model did not compromise the model's underlying integrity and purpose.

A third lesson learned from Dr. Golarz was how to develop a district climate and school climates that encouraged positive change, including the need to support individuals initiating new structures and programs. Positive change occurred much more naturally and easily when the foundations for change were properly established and included input from as many stakeholders as possible.

This process for cultivating a positive and productive district climate focused on bringing building leaders, district leaders, and the board together for extended, directed discussions about fundamental approaches to change based on the four core values dimension/area assessments (Empowerment/Involvement, Risk-taking, Curricular Flexibility, and Assessment).

This work was time-consuming and required everyone to be involved in the discussion, honest about their own views and values, and open to understanding the views and values of others. Too often, change is implemented without understanding the underlying value systems of the change agents. Leaders that take time to understand their own and others' views and values have powerful knowledge about the needs and desires of internal audiences and external stakeholders. This knowledge facilitates more effective and lasting change.

Finally, the development and implementation of a highly participatory model for decision-making required a clearly defined process. Developing awareness and consensus of core values is only one piece of the whole; the procedural details must also be well defined. Dr. Golarz's continued input was critical in keeping the district's implementation efforts moving forward. Development of clear, functional procedures were the result of steady, purposeful work over time. Guidelines were developed to clarify when proposals for change should be driven by the board, the superintendent, and/or by principals. These guidelines and procedures defined and clarified each leadership group's role as change agents. Increased role clarity minimized clashes between leadership groups and enabled changes to occur that were supported appropriately by all three leadership entities.

The work with Dr. Golarz also resulted in several other valuable lessons learned about bringing in an external expert over a long period of time. One of the most valuable lessons learned was the importance of continuing introductions and statements of purpose on a regular basis. New employees and board members were not familiar with Dr. Golarz or his role in the district. The need for regular introductions and statements of purpose were especially important after Dr. Golarz's work became well established and was no longer a new and heated topic of discussion. In addition, Dr. Golarz's role in the district shifted and changed over time. Acknowledging these new roles was just as important and urgent as introducing and acknowledging earlier roles had been.

Over time, it became important to strategically introduce Dr. Golarz to various groups to maximize the effects of his work. Dr. Golarz possesses a unique blend of talents, not the least of which is his ability as a motivational speaker. Occasionally, he was asked to give motivational presentations to a variety of district audiences, including union leaders, teachers, new teachers, and special area staff. The senior leadership team determined when, how, and why to introduce Dr. Golarz to additional district audiences. This team was aware of Dr. Golarz's strengths and considered having him speak when planning upcoming professional development events.

Dr. Golarz facilitated significant, lasting change in the district, which he described as "changing the fundamental architecture of the district." This change was accomplished by engaging the board, administrators, and teacher leaders in the long process of understanding their own core values and using them to empower these leaders at a level where they felt a sense of ownership while still being supported. By working with the district and the superintendent, the term "participatory leadership" came to mean the customized leadership protocol adopted in the district, which was a blend of site-based and central-office based leadership. Building leaders experienced a degree of management autonomy, but not at the expense of fundamental unifying district characteristics and protocols. Maintaining a degree of central office authority ensured equity, fairness, and a balanced and beneficial level of uniformity throughout the district.

Dr. Golarz worked with the school district from 1996 to 2008. He was initially hired to help the district develop a decision-making model that struck a workable balance between site-based leadership and central office leadership. As a result of Dr. Golarz's work, a customized version of participatory leadership was adopted that created a workable system of checks and balances between the board, central office administrators, and building administrators. The work with Dr. Golarz also helped these leadership groups to more clearly identify their leadership roles and to interact more effectively with one another.

As a result of the district's work with Dr. Golarz in developing the decision-making model, other district planning instruments were reviewed and revised to better align with the new understanding of the core values held by the leadership groups, teachers, and the community. The planning instruments that were developed, revised, and reviewed included three long-range plans, the district vision, and the district mission.

Although Dr. Golarz was hired to address the decision-making model, his work and influence had a far-reaching impact on the foundational structures of the district. A great deal of time with Dr. Golarz was spent in discussing and unpacking the values of district leadership groups, and analyzing the perceived values of the community. This work created deeper understanding among these leadership groups regarding areas where the school district and community were well aligned and where they were not. This information enabled the district to move forward more aggressively in some areas, while taking time to increase education and public interaction in other areas.

While the decision-making model worked well for new initiatives and implementations, it did not work so well to address existing and/or recurring problems and issues, many of which created a large amount of public tension. These hot-button issues required a different approach to problem-solving than the norm, including increased opportunities for public interaction. To address these issues, the district developed and adopted a public engagement model so that district decision making could include more awareness of the public's concerns and ideas about possible solutions and directions for next steps.

Dr. Golarz also played an important role as a personal advisor to the superintendent. Because he was familiar with district dynamics, yet was not personally vested in the district, he could offer the superintendent valuable insight, information, and direction in many areas. This role evolved over time as Dr. Golarz worked with the district and earned the superintendent's trust, as well as the trust of the board, administrative team, and teachers leaders.

In reflecting on the impact of Dr. Golarz's direction and guidance spanning a 12-year period, his influence as a targeted change agent became clear. Dr. Golarz began his journey with the district under a first-time superintendent with on year of experience in the district, who believed he and the district were ready to delve into the difficult work of making significant, fundamental improvements in the district over the long haul. Dr. Golarz ended his time with the district under the same superintendent, now an experienced veteran, who was still searching for ways to create better learning experiences for students in the district.

During Dr. Golarz's time with the district, increased federal involvement in education, most notably with No Child Left Behind (NCLB), an increased number of unfunded mandates, and increased revenue shortfalls brought a new host of problems and issues to address. Dr. Golarz was able to help the superintendent address these issues, both directly and indirectly, by maintaining a focus on the core values of the leadership groups, and helping new members of these leadership groups focus on their leadership roles so that the three groups (board, superintendent, and administrative team) could continue to work together through increasingly difficult political and economic times.

NOTES

1. This timeline is interesting in itself given that the tenure of the average superintendent, is significantly less than eight years. Thus, in many districts with regular superintendent turnover, it is reasonable to presume that these recurring issues will resurface and be new to the new superintendent. So, instead of moving forward and making progress with the issue, a great deal of time is spent rehashing the old issue to bring the new superintendent up to speed.

Chapter 3

Addressing Diversity Issues in the District

In the previous chapter, we reviewed the work of an expert who was hired to help the district implement large-scale foundational changes in the district-wide decision-making processes. Dr. Golarz served as a targeted change agent over the course of several years to help the district successfully implement the new processes. In addition, Dr. Golarz expanded his role to include advising the superintendent on a variety of issues in later years.

Obviously, Dr. Golarz represents only one example of the ways an external expert may offer unique benefits to a school district and/or superintendent. Sometimes, the expert's role is not to facilitate implementation of a new program or initiative, but to bring awareness to certain issues and to increase the level of urgency for district action, whatever that action may be. In this model, the expert will likely provide some suggestions and direction; however, the task of developing strategies, solutions, and action steps toward implementation is more likely in the hands of district personnel.

English and Steffy (1984) identify several conditions under which school districts may turn to external experts for help. One of the conditions English and Steffy describe is a lack of political strength:

> Some problems are so messy and complex that the client fears that if the problems were attacked internally, the ramifications and consequences might undo any positive impact of altering the structure or process. Therefore, a consultant is employed to "excuse" the organization from having to bear the burden of attacking itself. This prevents internal polarization from occurring between groups within the organization (p. 3).

In this context, "excuse" is not an abdication of responsibility; rather, it is the realization that there are certain issues in which school leaders may need the help of an external expert who is less vested in the district and more knowledgeable regarding the issue. Such experts help increase awareness of the problems and can lead the organization to appropriate solutions.

As the superintendent continued his tenure in the district, the issue of how to address the needs of a rapidly growing and increasingly diverse population was one such urgent, complex issue with political implications throughout the region. Despite the community's growing cultural diversity, the district did not have many of the resources for culturally diverse students as other nearby communities of similar or larger size.

Many staff members in the district recognized the urgency of the issue, especially as it related to the achievement gap between white students and non-white students. However, individual staff members did not necessarily know what to do, and appropriate district-wide support for these students was needed. The district hired an external expert to facilitate increased awareness of cultural differences and help with the development of action steps that would address the achievement gap and other issues related to increased cultural diversity in the district.

The late 1990s were a time of significant change in the district. While the teachers and staff were still 99 percent white, the number of minority students tripled in an eight-year period from 1994–95 to 2008–09. Not insignificantly, the number of students receiving free and reduced lunch in the district also tripled during this time period. In short, the demographics of the community and of the student populations were changing dramatically. Yet, many long-standing community members and members of the teaching staff were not fully aware of or sensitive to the implications of the new dynamics that were present in the city and the school district as a result of these significant population and economic shifts. Other members of the community and teaching staff who were aware that changes needed to occur and who advocated for change needed more knowledge, guidance, and support as well as a stronger voice in leadership in order to make lasting change occur.

In 2000, the superintendent believed that the timing was right to highlight issues involving diversity within the context of student achievement. He decided to hire an expert to help address the pressing cultural issues facing the school district, which could be described as a historically isolated, white middle-class district that needed to be more aware of cultural issues facing school systems in the twenty-first century. The superintendent believed that, rather than addressing the issue of cultural diversity personally and directly, a more effective approach would be to hire the right external expert to help guide and assist district personnel through the struggle that would enable the district as a whole to better accept, understand, and respond to the needs of diverse students. Dr. Evert recalls:

> I remember Dr. Odom from my time [working] in a neighboring district, and I heard about his book and his work with other urban school districts in the state. I knew he was working with other districts and businesses, and his familiarity with the dynamics between our district and the neighboring district made him my first choice to address this issue.

Dr. Odom is an experienced cultural diversity management expert for corporations, school systems, and universities. He served as an English teacher in a neighboring district from 1969 to 1973, as director of the human relations department in one of the state's largest school districts, and as a middle school principal in the same large school district. Odom earned his B.A. from a historically black college in the South, his M.S. and Ph.D. in Educational Administration from the University of Wisconsin-Madison. His book, *Saving Black America: An Economic Plan for Civil Rights* (2001) focuses on the economic benefits of providing minority children with the best and most rigorous education available and the importance of economics ("the color green") in closing the achievement gap between blacks and whites. A review of his book relates the following:

> The notion of bridging the gap between blacks and whites with green, the color of money, is not new. But Odom's book is an especially cogent presentation of why an economic strategy for pursuing civil rights is black America's best hope—and of how such a strategy can be executed. Black American leaders would be smart to read Odom's advice. Protest and legislation still have roles to play in combating racism. But strengthening black families and communities from within, economically, can, as Odom says, "create a better set of possibilities" (Wisconsin State Journal March 13, 2002).

Budget issues significantly affected the process of hiring Dr. Odom. The funds for this engagement came from the superintendent's discretionary budget specifically set aside for items such as external experts. The board was informed of Dr. Odom's hire, but the superintendent did not seek formal board approval for the hire. While the superintendent and other key administrative personnel supported the need for hiring Dr. Odom to fill a 200-hour per year position (25 days per year), financial realities and budget shortfalls in the district resulted in a contract for 4 to 5 days per year at $2,000 per day (not to exceed $10,000 per year). As a result of this arrangement,

Dr. Odom's time needed to be carefully planned and used very efficiently in order to be effective. This work started during the 2000–2001 school year.

Dr. John Odom visited the district three to four times per year for eight years from 2000 to 2008. During that time, Dr. Odom addressed several issues in the district related to cultural diversity, with a focus on three main areas: (1) understanding and improving student achievement among minority students, (2) recruiting and retaining minority teachers and staff members, and (3) improving racial relations between our school district and the neighboring district, which included an intense athletic conference rivalry. Dr. Odom's work with the district helped to find new and creative solutions to problems that were well known but seemingly unsolvable.

The issue of the relations between our district and the neighboring district merit some background in order to fully understand the dynamics. The two communities that contain these districts are the largest communities in the county with populations in the 40,000 to 60,000 range. They are geographically very close together and are economically, politically, and culturally tied regardless of their individual similarities and differences. The school districts from these communities are interconnected with especially fierce athletic competition but also a high level of cooperation between the districts' staff and administrations.

One of the most striking differences in the two communities is the degree of cultural diversity in each. The neighboring district is far more culturally diverse than the subject district of this book, and that fact has resulted in significant racial tensions over the years, particularly among students at athletic competitions. Dr. Odom's familiarity with both districts and the dynamics at play between the two made him the best choice for working with the district's diversity issues.

UNDERSTANDING AND IMPROVING STUDENT ACHIEVEMENT

In order to address the achievement gap between white and minority students in the district, it was decided that Dr. Odom's efforts would at first be most beneficially directed toward working with school principals as part of the long-range diversity efforts in the district. Dr. Odom held roundtable discussions with small groups of principals to discuss, dialogue, and identify proactive steps that could be taken to improve learning for all students in general and minority students in particular. Principals were able to take the information from the roundtable back to their schools and work with staff on individual school improvement plans to help close the achievement gap.

It is important to note that initially, there were (not unexpectedly) various levels of acceptance and resistance to the message that Dr. Odom brought to the district. Some administrators did not want to be told that they had to do something additional or special for a certain group of students. Lindsay, Robins & Terrell (2009) describe a "cultural proficiency continuum," including six points that "indicate unique ways of seeing and responding to differences" (p. 6).

The third of these points, and placed along the unhealthy part of the continuum is "cultural blindness." Cultural blindness is defined as "not noticing or acknowledging the culture of others and ignoring the discrepant experiences of cultures within the schools; treating everyone the same way without recognizing the needs that require differentiated interaction" (p. 6). As a community and as a school district, Dr. Odom and the Superintendent observed that the district existed in a culturally blind environment. As one principal noted in an interview with the local newspaper, "closing the achievement gap means using 'not necessarily the same middle-class approach we're accustomed to'" (October 15, 2005).

As a result of Dr. Odom's work, each school developed a yearly human relations plan, including a report, which became part of the school improvement plan and focused on opening dialogue and incorporating a variety of topics focused on minority student achievement into staff development meetings. Topics covered in these meetings included attendance and behavior, the effects of stereotyping, special education placements, and participation in advanced placement classes. Identifying these topics was the result of the district's work with Dr. Odom.

Some of Dr. Odom's time was also spent with teaching staff at these staff development meetings. Small group dialogue was also encouraged because it was felt that smaller groups would be a more comfortable setting for discussion. For example, during one staff development meeting, Dr. Odom answered questions from the staff about a wide variety of issues related to the achievement gap and cultural diversity. Below is an excerpt from that meeting, which serves to illustrate ways in which staff members grappled with cultural diversity issues:

Question:	Is there a difference between rural and urban poverty in relationship to the stereotypes we are assigning to students in poverty?
Dr. Odom:	None really. The world has gotten so small. For example, demeaning words, they are used in black and white, urban and rural cultures.
Question:	How do you help break a cycle of generational poverty when parents don't understand that what they do, say, and permit their child to do has consequences at school?

Dr. Odom:	We must include parents, pastors, and community agencies. We must have frank discussions. We need parenting groups. Perhaps a diversity council. Fortune 500 companies have them, and they serve as advisors. Listen to viewpoints.
Question:	Why does there appear to be an acceptance among students of poverty and color to often resort to violence when they feel slighted or disrespected by other children? What are some tips in dealing with this behavior?
Dr. Odom:	It is regional and socioeconomic, not cultural. You could go to New York and get beat up just as easy by a white, Irish kid. We must encourage kids to think it's tougher to focus on academics than fighting. Encourage them to distinguish themselves in other ways (music, academics, art, etc.).
Question:	In the classroom, how can you be consistent with consequences when not everyone has the same resources/values in their homes?
Dr. Odom:	It's not the home. Have consistent rules in the school and classroom.
Question:	Do students of different cultural backgrounds still deal with exile from their group if they move toward the mainstream culture regarding the value of education? If so, how can educators assist in easing this peer pressure?
Dr. Odom:	Excellence is excellence. Excellence does not always equate to being white. We must explain to kids just because you achieve doesn't mean you are white. We can't allow one culture to claim excellence. Tell students they will survive. No, they are not trying to be white, they are trying to be excellent. White people don't own excellence.

Dr. Odom's work with the district was very helpful in raising awareness and creating urgency in addressing the achievement gap issue in the district. However, as mentioned earlier, specific solutions and follow-up were left to the district to develop and implement. Dr. Odom provided suggestions and direction, but the district took responsibility for decision-making and implementation.

District personnel actively sought Dr. Odom's suggestions and direction as an expert on diversity issues. For example, during the 2003–2004 school year, the curriculum director made a request to Dr. Odom asking for "3 to 5 specific approaches to support the learning needs of the district's high achieving students of color." Dr. Odom provided specific suggestions with explanations, including the following: (1) a collaboration or coordination point (such as a Human Relations Council); (2) culturally sensitive curricula; (3) culturally sensitive instructional methods; (4) exposure (to areas that reveal talents and gifts); (5) role models;

(6) parental involvement; (7) parental education; and (8) accountability and rewards (to staff members who "place more emphasis on diversity" than others).

An important issue in the district that impacted the diversity initiative was the high turnover of curriculum directors during Dr. Odom's first four years working with the district. By the fourth year of Dr. Odom's work, a new curriculum director (the fourth person in six years) was hired, and she placed greater emphasis on student achievement among minority students.

As a result of hiring a curriculum director who would serve the district for five years, the urgency to address the achievement gap was increased, which in turned resulted in more action. Dr. Odom used an approach that relied on data to drive action. He would regularly ask for a variety of achievement data for different racial groups. In one such analysis, the curriculum department examined and analyzed data and strategies with minority students (largely African American and Hispanic) based on 2003–2004 test scores in grades 4, 6, and 10 in math and reading. In a letter from the district to Dr. Odom, the curriculum director states that

> [we] have looked at our WKCE scores[1] (past three years). It is quite clear that there is an achievement gap between our Black and Hispanic students compared to our White students. We don't feel that it is necessary for us to have a prediction study done knowing that we have a lot of work to do. . . . The gaps start becoming very visible at the 8th and 10th grade. The data for 8th and 10th grades are disaggregated by building.

In addition to this candid assessment, the curriculum director's report includes the following questions: (1) how do we close the achievement gap within 6 years, (2) what action steps are other school districts and communities taking, (3) how does the district help teachers better manage classrooms, (4) how should minority student be referred for additional services, and (5) how do we gain community support for these efforts?

While Dr. Odom kept promoting the need to close the achievement gap, it took a dedicated effort for action on the part of the district for change to occur. Dr. Odom laid the foundation for readiness and gathered significant and useful data from the new curriculum director's predecessor. The new curriculum director was able to use this data and Dr. Odom's suggestions to develop a plan for action. After four years, the real work of change was underway.

As mentioned earlier, Dr. Odom suggested in 2003–2004 that the district consider creating a Human Relations Council that could serve as a collaboration or coordination point. From 2004–2007, a central office group consisting of the superintendent, curriculum director, and a curriculum coordinator would meet to review, plan, and implement human relations activities that included scheduling Dr. Odom's time in the district. This group met three to four times a year, usually in the summer, fall, and spring. While this structure kept the diversity initiative alive, it alone was not sufficient to effectively move the district forward in a proactive and focused way.

Box 3.1 District Diversity Committee

This advisory committee keeps detailed minutes at each meeting, and a typical agenda includes five to ten items. Attendance at these committees averages about 20 people, with nearly half of the attendees being community members and student representatives. Listed below is a sample of topics covered at these meetings:

November, 2007
- Review of data pertaining to truancy of minority students
- How to address issues of Jewish holidays and the district calendar

February, 2008
- Review of mission and vision statement for the Diversity Committee
- Update on progress of program entitled "Courageous Conversations"
- Discussion of after school program for Hispanic students

April, 2008
- Introduction of Multicultural Teacher Scholarship "grow your own" program
- Review of data related to English Language Learner program from 2005–06 to present

September, 2008
- Minority performance on ACT tests
- Recruiting staff of color

October, 2008
- Dr. Odom addressed the group and discussed as related to the committee
  - strategic planning, vision, and mission statements
- Student activities, including college visits, multicultural days, etc.

November, 2008
- Progress of "grow your own" multicultural scholarship for future teachers
  - open to district minority students

January, 2009
- Need for a minority peer mentoring program
- Review of data regarding advanced placement courses
  - test results as related to minority student participation
- Possible participation of staff in "diversity circles" model under direction of Studer Group coach
- Student activities highlighted

February, 2009
- Review drafts of vision/mission statements according to Dr. Odom's criteria

March, 2009
- Review new staff development plan
  - new teachers required to attend two full days of diversity training
- Review of activities from secondary schools' human relations clubs

October 2009
- Restructure diversity efforts to better coordinate and reduce duplication

January, 2010
- Reading instruction and test scores for minority high school students
  - steps to address concerns were discussed

March 2010
- Review English Language Learners program
- Review of District Diversity Committee and District Equity Leadership Team
- Review of school-level programs

The need to move toward a more structured and forceful planning and monitoring approach developed over the next three years. In 2007, Dr. Odom strongly encouraged the superintendent to start a district-level Diversity Committee. The committee was intended to be a clearinghouse for diversity; that is, the committee would serve as a single place where issues related to diversity would be discussed and addressed. This committee would serve in an advisory capacity to the superintendent. The committee was formed in the fall of 2007 and continues to meet and deliberate as of the fall of 2010. The activities of the Diversity Committee are outlined in Textbox 3.1.

RECRUITING AND RETAINING CULTURALLY DIVERSE TEACHERS AND STAFF

Another key issue regarding cultural diversity in the district was the makeup of the school staff. Teachers and staff were virtually all white. When asked for specific suggestions about which next steps to pursue, Dr. Odom provided the following suggestions regarding role models:

> There is often a shortage of educators of color. This problem is exacerbated for boys of color in elementary school—a stage where boys are forming their identities both as males and as students. Elementary schools tend to be White female dominated with few, if any, males, let alone men of color. Nonetheless, there typically are men of color in the community who would be very interested in helping when they are invited to do so. They should be invited.

District personnel concurred with Dr. Odom regarding the importance of role models in students' development, and that a culturally diverse population should interact with culturally diverse staff and community members. As a result of Dr. Odom's work, the district cultivated several successful partnerships with local African-American men who served as role models to many boys in the district.

To increase the number of minority teachers in the district, several recruitment efforts have been attempted. It should be noted at the outset of this section that, while some efforts yielded a temporary increase in culturally diverse teachers, these increases were short-lived. After working in the district for no more than a couple of years, all of these recruited teachers moved out of the district. It is also worth noting that neighboring communities with greater cultural diversity experienced similar difficulties diversifying their teaching staff using active recruiting techniques.

The first of these efforts involved attending recruiting fairs in nearby urban areas with large diverse populations. For several years, the district human resources director attended these fairs, actively recruiting culturally diverse teachers. However, this approach did not yield positive results. During the time that the district was actively recruiting, urban areas were offering substantial signing bonuses to culturally diverse teachers. The district was viewed by the teacher candidates from larger urban areas as being mostly white with limited social opportunities. Moving to such a district to teach meant that candidates were giving up the lifestyle and sense of community to which they were accustomed. Many single teachers perceived limited opportunities for dating and engaging in a social life with people of their own cultural heritage.

In the early 2000s, a nearby large urban area in a neighboring state with a substantial non-white population laid off a significant number of teachers. These layoffs resulted in a combined effort by the school district and the neighboring district to recruit culturally diverse teachers from the urban district. This effort led to accusations by local school officials in the large urban district that these communities were trying to steal teachers. The district learned the hard way that the process of diversifying the school staff was not as smooth or straightforward as it first seemed.

Another related effort to hire African American teachers was undertaken when the district agreed to partner with an African American recruiter. This recruiter agreed to an arrangement whereby fees would be collected by the recruiter only when candidates were actually hired by the district. This agreement lasted three years and during that time she recruited no teachers, although a few African American teachers were hired in the district through other means.

Other efforts have also been undertaken to diversify the teaching staff in the district. Education, business, and religious leaders throughout the county organized to discuss efforts to improve minority recruiting using a hiring model presented in a workshop at a technical college centrally located between the district and neighboring district. The organization consisted of a racially diverse group and met at the technical college on a regular basis for four years. While discussions were worthwhile and important, implementation of the model never took hold and hiring practices were not effectively changed.

During the 2007–2008 school year, a new approach to diversifying the teaching staff was started. This approach consisted of a privately funded and district approved scholarship program designed to support the teacher education of local culturally diverse. Students in the district can receive partial or full scholarships to college in order to become teachers with the understanding that they would return to the district and teach for at least three years. The program is managed and funded completely outside of the school district. Identifying and articulating the specifics of this program has been somewhat challenging, and the success of the program has yet to be determined.

Dr. Odom's work with the district helped develop awareness of cultural issues and develop a purposeful plan of action to increase student achievement among culturally diverse students. The complex and highly-charged nature of diversity issues are challenging at best. While some progress was made with the help of Dr. Odom and others, the district is still trying to close the achievement gap. The reality is that efforts to close achievement gaps and provide more support for diverse student populations are ongoing and continuous, and progress is slow. However, the positive effects of Dr. Odom's work continue in the district. Teachers and staff are more aware of the needs of diverse student populations and are better prepared to provide appropriate support to all students.

IMPROVING RACIAL RELATIONS BETWEEN THE DISTRICT AND THE NEIGHBORING DISTRICT

The superintendent relied on Dr. Odom's advice and expertise to help negotiate a partnership with a neighboring district to implement and continue programs designed to improve racial relations between the two communities. Racial tensions had existed between the two communities for decades. Our subject district was largely a white, middle class community that relied on industry to maintain a robust middle-class standard of living. The neighboring district had a much more racially diverse population and was considered less economically stable and by some, less desirable.

This perception has changed dramatically in recent decades. The closure of industry in the subject district has shattered its economic base and self-image as a community, while the neighboring district is home to a small, elite private college and has experienced a recent influx of large business, creating a surge of desirable urban culture and industry. As a result of these shifts, both communities appeal to many of the same populations, both economically and socially.

Notwithstanding the shifts in economy and demographics, racial tensions between the two communities remained high in the 1990s and early 2000s. These tensions would often erupt among students at middle and high school athletic events between these two rival schools. Because Dr. Odom was very familiar with the cultures of both communities and both school districts, his input and advice was helpful in facilitating an active, working partnership between the two districts. This partnership resulted in real progress toward improving racial relations between the two communities.

An important piece of this school district partnership was that it was not in name only; rather, it included concrete actions and efforts that resulted in long-term improved relationships between the two school districts. Both superintendents had a shared vision and commitment to addressing the needs of culturally diverse students and a positive working relationship that helped sustain the efforts over several years. In addition, the following three action steps made the partnership work: 1) shared administrative training; 2) formal student/school exchanges; and 3) the creation and adoption of formal procedures and policies for athletic events.

Dr. Odom met with administrators from both school districts an average of twice a year. His sessions focused on a wide range of staff development topics, including the need for special emphasis on improving economic conditions for poor families (with special emphasis on culturally diverse families), factors that may inhibit academic achievement in culturally diverse students, and the need for culturally sensitive curricula for all students. As Dr. Evert recalls:

> Dr. Odom was very helpful to me because our district did not have the diversity resources that the other district did. He brought a different frame or perspective from which to consider the entire issue. Dr. Odom encouraged economic development in order to facilitate racial equality. He believed that staff members and community members are less defensive if the issue is framed in relation to earning power as opposed to instilling guilt or using other past barriers that prohibit rather than foster open discussion.

In his work facilitating the two-district partnership, Dr. Odom promoted the concept of framing the issue of diversity and the achievement gap by using data in order to minimize the emotionality that frequently occurs when racial issues are addressed. He served as neutral figure and was accepted by both districts for his knowledge and experience in dealing with diversity issues throughout the state. By focusing on economic issues, Dr. Odom did not divert the discussion away from its racial focus, but rather framed it in terms of what was needed in order to realize increased achievement among culturally diverse students.

LESSONS LEARNED

Dr. Odom reminded us of the need to continually promote the message of acknowledging and encouraging diversity, and his work focused largely on addressing the achievement gap between white and non-white students. He helped the district frame the achievement gap issue by introducing the concept of the economics, which helped the district take important first steps in closing that gap. Dr. Odom stressed the importance of using data to discuss the issue of minority student achievement in order to recognize areas of strength and pinpoint specific areas of weakness. This approach resulted in more efficient and effective methods of raising achievement in weaker areas. While the use of data seems relatively easy and straightforward, the district learned that it can take a long time go from data gathering and analysis to instructional action steps.

Probably the most important lesson that the district learned from Dr. Odom is that the time between initially addressing an issue and seeing tangible results in terms of increased student achievement can take much longer than one might think. Dr. Odom worked with the district for eight years, and it took nearly half of that time to get many of the foundational action steps associated with his work implemented. That being said, the positive effects of Dr. Odom's work on student achievement continue today, over two years after Dr. Odom's last formal consultation with the district. Minority student achievement has increased in the past five years.

In reflecting further on the issues of cultural diversity and the achievement gap, and after speaking with other superintendents throughout the state, this long timeline for implementation and results appears to mirror the timelines that other districts experience when addressing diversity issues. While that statement may sound defensive or like an excuse, it is not meant to be so.

Simply stated, finding answers to issues involving cultural diversity are far more complex than identifying the problems and seeking appropriate solutions. The district learned through the entire experience of addressing the achievement gap issue proactively that different issues require different amounts of time, resources, and efforts. Another difficult lesson learned was that results and solutions do not always correlate directly to the time, resources, and efforts put into them. Sometimes, in order to see even small successes with some issues, a steady stream of resources and efforts over time are essential.

The final lesson learned from Dr. Odom is that when working on a difficult issue over many years, it is important to receive a periodic overview of progress from the expert along with his or her recommendations for future actions. This process can rejuvenate the effort, and is especially important when feelings of stagnation and frustration with the lack of progress on an issue start to become apparent.

In 2008, the superintendent and curriculum director charged Odom "with the task of developing a report that represents the district's efforts and that provides recommendations for moving forward" (memo, July 14, 2008). The resulting report detailed the progress that had been made on the initiative to that point and provided approximately 20 specific action steps that could help the district move forward to address diversity issues more effectively in the coming years.

The report provided an accurate summary that could be shared with staff, and provided a plan for future actions. Probably the most notable result of this document is the establishment and continuance of the Superintendent's Diversity Committee. It should be noted that this document was created toward the end of Dr. Odom's tenure with the district at a time when the current superintendent was contemplating retirement and setting the stage for his predecessor.

Dr. Odom served a very specific, intermittent, specialized role in the district and was uniquely qualified to offer direction and advice. One condition English and Steffy identify that can require the help of an external consultant is lack of credibility:

> [One] reason consultants are employed is to reinforce facts or trends identified by top management, but which for one reason or another lack credibility to various constituencies within an organization. The consultant possesses credibility and is able to make progress for management that would otherwise not be possible (p. 9).

The fact of the matter was that the superintendent was a veteran white male in a position of authority. While one of the major goals for his tenure in the district was to improve student achievement for culturally diverse students, it was challenging at best to directly facilitate the open dialogue required as a first step toward positive change given his position and ethnicity.

Dr. Odom had a wealth of experience and knowledge in the field of cultural diversity, and the fact that he was African-American helped some administrators and teaching staff members overcome their discomfort about having a frank, open discussion about racial issues in a mixed-race audience. He openly talked about the achievement gap among young African American males, a gap that was borne out all too clearly in district testing data. He also facilitated a conversation that was aimed at framing the conversation and action steps in positive terms as benefiting all students in the district, making it a better place for all students to learn.

NOTES

1. The Wisconsin Knowledge and Concept Exam (WKCE) is a state test administered to grades 4, 8, and 10. This assessment is used to measure compliance with academic standards established through No Child Left Behind (NCLB).

Chapter 4

Using External Experts to Address a Wide Range of Issues

The previous two chapters explored two contexts in which external experts served as valuable resources. One context involved foundational cultural and systems changes in the district that took place over a long period of time. The expert worked with the board, administrative team, and teacher values to assess and align the vision and mission of the district, and as a result, structural changes in the district decision-making processes occurred.

The other context involved efforts to change relationships and educational approaches to increase awareness of cultural differences and to close the achievement gap. This issue was very sensitive and politically charged. The expert worked with administrators, teachers, and staff to facilitate discussion. He also provided useful suggestions for action that did help the district serve all of its student populations more effectively.

There are, of course, several other contexts in which the use of external experts is desirable and beneficial. While we make no claim to cover all such contexts in this book, the six experts discussed in this book represent distinctly different contexts, because each expert has different areas of expertise, roles, and outcomes for the district. In this chapter, we will look at three different external experts that represent three different contexts in which external experts can be used beneficially.

The first expert is a specialist in school fianance. The district was fortunate to employ a very competent financial officer; however, even the best financial officer may benefit from assistance when the district needs certain complex financial services performed. Whether or not he or she has the necessary expertise, the finance officer may not have the time or other resources in order to handle some complex transactions effectively. For example, managing district liabilities and large referendum funds requires precise timing and full consideration of all the issues and available options in order to develop an acceptable array of choices for board consideration.

The second expert is a specialist in the area of school safety as part of the administration of a federal grant. The grant funds covered the expert's fees, and he was engaged to provide a full range of services that helped the district reach the goals articulated in the grant proposal. These services included assessments, training, and simulations as well as serving in a traditional consulting capacity.

The third expert was a one-time presenter in the district in the area of generational differences. Bringing an expert in for a one-time visit has received a great deal of criticism from teachers and education specialists (Riley, 1993; Cooper, 2009) because there can be a lack of follow up and implementation. However, it can be an effective way to increase staff knowledge on some topics if the presentation is complete and focused. Inviting personnel from other districts and involving the local media can extend the expert's impact to further increase the benefits for the district.

CAROL WIRTH: SCHOOL FINANCE

In the area of school finance, school districts typically hire a business manager, financial director, CFO, or some other individual with expertise in the field of managing financial matters. These individuals are usually generalists, with broad-based knowledge about a variety of district operational concerns that may include transportation, building and grounds maintenance, or even technology in addition to budgeting and finance.

However, situations sometimes arise where an external expert can be of benefit—for example, certain complex financial transactions or determining financial direction. Referendums (bond sale coordination), pension liabilities, debt consolidation, and debt payoff are the types of issues where the district financial officer may benefit from the help of an external expert. These issues are large in scope and scale, and many millions of dollars are at stake. Having an external consultant come in and review, analyze, advise, and educate can help guide the board toward financial decisions that are consistent with the district's mission and the community's values.

To assist the district with challenging financial issues, Carol Wirth, President of Wisconsin Public Finance Professionals, LLC was hired on a regular basis. Ms. Wirth was first hired in the mid-1980s and continues to serve the district at this time. Ms. Wirth has served the district under two business directors and three superintendents. She acted primarily as an advisor to the business director and comptroller, meeting with each approximately once a month. She would meet with the business director, superintendent and/or board approximately three times per year, depending on the issues she was addressing at the time.

It is interesting to note that the financial arrangement between Ms. Wirth and the district involved payment almost entirely on a commission basis. For example, when she worked on the issuance of bonds as part of securing referendum funds for high school renovations in 2007–2008, she made a percentage of the amount of money she was able to save the district in securing an interest rate less than the projected amount. On rare occasions, when Ms. Wirth conducted a workshop or other event for the board, she would be paid a small stipend for her additional time out of a departmental discretionary fund.

Ms Wirth was hired primarily to assist district personnel in the management of bond funds related to building referendums and to help the district manage post employment benefits. Both of these items required a large amount of time and detail-oriented work. In addition, they required specialized expertise. For all of these reasons, it was not practical, nor prudent for the district business director to handle these items alone.

In less than a 10-year span, the public approved three school district facilities referendums. The first was in 1997 for $21.7 million. These funds enabled the district to build a new elementary school, remodel two other elementary schools, and implement a comprehensive technology plan in the district. The second referendum in 2004 was for $17 million, and was used to renovate five elementary schools. The third referendum was in 2006 for $70.9 million (the largest school referendum ever passed in the state at the time) and was used to rebuild and renovate the two high schools in the community.

For each of these referendums, bonds were issued to realize capital funds for the projects. Managing the issuance of these bonds required both strategic and technical expertise in addition to time. Ms. Wirth and the business director worked together to ensure that the district was properly showcased in order to receive the best possible bond ratings, and ultimately, the lowest possible interest rates on the debt. Ms. Wirth also addressed the board during critical junctures throughout the process so that the board would be aware of the district's bond ratings, what interest rates were projected for the bonds, the process for issuing bonds, and other relevant issues related to the financing of the referendums.

The other issues that Ms. Wirth addressed on a regular basis were a variety of post-employment benefit issues, including pensions and mandatory payments to the state retirement system. These financial liabilities were ongoing and very costly to the district, especially on a "pay as you go" basis. Because Ms. Wirth consulted for several school districts on this issue, she was very knowledgeable regarding the options available to achieve the district's financial goals.

One of the reasons that Ms. Wirth's services were so valuable on this subject is because choosing the best option for structuring these liability payments required careful analysis and consideration. Some districts chose to pay off obligations and liabilities sooner with larger payments up front, saving large amounts of interest in future years, while other districts chose to keep the payments as low as possible for the present with the understanding that payments would continue longer and accrue more interest. Ms. Wirth was able to analyze a district's needs and abilities and recommend a payment strategy that fit the values of the board and the fiscal resources of the district.

Ms. Wirth was occasionally asked to assist the board on one-time, politically sensitive financial items. The board greatly benefited from this independent perspective. One such issue was the general fund balance. The Wisconsin Department of Public Instruction (DPI) describes fund balance as the following:

> All school districts have a General Fund, and may have one or more other funds to account for specific activities. For example, special education activities are accounted for in the Special Education Fund. . . . The difference between the fund's assets and liabilities equals the "fund balance." A positive fund balance represents a financial resource available to finance expenditures of a following fiscal period. A deficit fund balance can only be recovered by having revenues exceed expenditures in a following fiscal period. . . . Administrators and board members need to understand what a fund balance is and its importance in budgeting decisions. A common misconception is that fund balance is a cash account and therefore corresponds to the district's bank balance. . . . A portion of the fund may be committed. . . . Fund balance is "surplus" only to the extent that it has not been committed (Retrieved October 30, 2010 from http://dpi.state.wi.us/sfs/fundbal.html).

DPI does not specify a dollar amount for fund balance. What they do suggest is that general fund balance should contain "an amount sufficient that short term borrowing for cash flow could be avoided and would also allow the district to set aside sufficient assets to realize its longer range goals" (Ibid.).

The general fund balance was and is considered to be an important barometer of district financial health, and the board monitored it very closely. The general fund balance is also money with which the board has some discretion. That is, the board may choose to use general fund balance to finance certain projects, programs, or initiatives, or it may choose to use it for unanticipated expenditures. For example, the board voted to approve construction of a wall behind one high school to act as a sound barrier for the nearby residents, which was funded using the general fund balance. The rule of thumb with general fund balance is that it should be used only for one-time expenditures (not recurring), and the balance in the account should remain at a level that reflects the district's overall positive financial health.

Certain board members and the business director would sometimes be at odds regarding the general fund balance, how much should be in it, and what it should be used for, if at all. Therefore, having an independent, knowledgeable, trustworthy, and proven third party come in and provide professional development to board members regarding the general fund balance was more appropriate than having such a session conducted by an internal person. In addition, yearly turnover created the need to educate new board members regarding certain fiscal aspects of district management. It was often more politically acceptable for both the board and the administration to hear sensitive financial information from a neutral third party.

As a result of the district's management of the general fund balance, including the work done by Ms. Wirth, the district was able to meet all payroll and bill obligations without borrowing funds and paying interest on the borrowed money. These obligations were met even as the state continually delayed its payments to school districts and other districts were indeed forced to borrow funds at times to meet payroll.

Mr. Doug Bunton, former business director, described Ms. Wirth's work with the district as being "comprehensive, thorough, complete, and clear" (personal interview, October 18, 2010). The board indicated that they valued her time and expertise also. Her financial services filled an important and urgent need in the district that required specialized, time-sensitive, yet intermittent attention. Ms. Wirth's work for the district helped the district maintain its good financial health and credit rating, and helped the district capitalize on it for the benefit of students and the community.

A complete discussion of district issues surrounding the general fund balance is described in Textboxes 4.1 and 4.2. This discussion illustrates the board's struggle to maintain an appropriate fund balance while using the funds on occasion for important one-time district expenditures. Ms. Wirth and the board workshop helped the board to establish guidelines for maintaining and using the fund balance that were aligned with the values of the district and the community.

Box 4.1 Issues Surrounding General Fund Balance and the Board of Education

The state funding formula during the years covered in this book consisted of three components:

- An average of two-thirds state funding per district
- A minimum salary and fringe benefit offer to teachers of 3.8 percent which, if offered by the board must be accepted by the teachers (repealed in 2009)
- A cap on revenues a district could receive, which was based in large part on student enrollment history.

As a result of the state funding formula, districts experiencing stable or declining enrollments faced decreasing revenues. Stable or decreasing enrollments shrunk the revenue cap, which meant that the maximum allowable taxation rate without going to a referendum would not keep pace with a 3.8 percent minimum teacher raise while maintaining all services and programs at the current year's level. The district faced this problem when enrollments began a slight decline beginning in the 2003–2004 school year. Each year, budget deliberations became more difficult and tense. Budget cuts were made and all aspects of the budget received careful board scrutiny.

It is in the context described above that a healthy general fund balance becomes a tempting source to tap. The ample fund balance created a dilemma for the board regarding appropriate uses for the money in the account and the amount that should be allocated to the account. Board members, school staff, and the general public needed to understand the purposes of the general fund balance as it related to the bigger picture of school finance. In June 2008, the board scheduled a special study session to learn about the general fund balance, which included an in-depth presentation by Ms. Wirth.

During this time, the board was not necessarily comfortable with the assessments made by only one expert. Both the business director and Ms. Wirth agreed that for this particular board session, it would be beneficial to bring in additional experts to offer different perspectives on the general fund balance for board consideration. Two additional experts presented at this board session. One expert was a benefits specialist and one was a CPA. The benefits specialist spoke about the relationship between the fund balance and the district self-funded insurance benefit plan and related costs.

The CPA was brought in to confirm the importance of the interrelationships between fund balance and other components of the district financial picture. In many ways, the CPA verified what Ms. Wirth conveyed to the board, but offered a slightly different perspective on the subject.

2008 was not the first time that the board needed to discuss issues regarding the general fund balance, and a similar workshop was also held in 2001. The general fund balance was also part of board financial workshops held in 2002, 2003, 2004, 2006, and 2007. These study sessions dealt with unfunded pension liabilities, referendum bond ratings, and Wisconsin Act 11, all of which included discussion of the general fund balance as an integral part of addressing these other issues.

Box 4.2   Board of Education Fund Balance Workshop

The focus of the study session was to stress the importance of a specific strategy for managing the general fund balance. Along with her presentation, Ms. Wirth prepared a three-page document for the board entitled "Fund Balance and the Rating Process." In it, she articulated the following reasons for developing and adopting a formal strategy for the general fund balance:

- Adherence to a fund balance strategy is viewed as being proactive and reflects positively on management. Factors to be included in the final determination of reserve balances include the level of budgetary fixed costs, historical delays in adoption of state budgets (determination of state aids), proximity to operating limits, statutory limitations on revenues (revenue limit), timing on reception of major revenue sources such as state aids or tax levy.
- Fund balance is an important consideration in establishing financial flexibility in times of economic slowdown. Fund balance policy is the management tool that plays a critical role in monitoring results for successfully managed governments.
- The district's historical fund balance is measured by the total general fund balance, designated and unreserved fund balance, and as a percentage of total general fund revenues and general/special revenue funds.
- Financial statistics include the percentages of general fund balance to either total expenditures or total revenues. Standard & Poor's median for AA rated issuers as unreserved general fund balance is 16.7 percent of general fund expenditures. In addition, historical financial practices of the district

are noted in credit reports as having an informal policy of maintaining a general fund balance of no more than three months' expenditures.

Ms. Wirth's contribution to the session was to present issues related to the general fund balance from the perspective of the district's bond rating in the marketplace. She stated that "[t]he District's bond ratings are an assessment of the credit risks" (minutes from the study session). Ms. Wirth recommended a written fund balance policy to help strengthen the bond rating. She also indicated that bond rating companies looked at how districts use their fund balance money (e.g., one-time expenditures) and how the fund balance can carry districts through difficult financial periods.

Ms. Wirth made the following specific recommendations to the board:

- Establish a formal, written general fund balance policy, including setting forth acceptable uses of the fund balance above the policy reserve levels.
- Maintain a stable financial profile of two to three months' expenditures.
- Maintain an unreserved-designated general fund balance of 17 percent to 19 percent of the ensuing year's budgeted general fund and special revenue fund expenditures for financial flexibility.

After all material was presented, the board engaged Ms. Wirth, the business director, and the superintendent in a question and answer session. This board study session is an excellent example of a district-lead, expert-based presentation on a complex financial issue, which in this instance was the general fund balance. By working with an expert, these elected public officials gained a deeper understanding of the uses and effects of the general fund balance, which helped them make better policies and decisions regarding management of the fund.

KEN TRUMP: SCHOOL SAFETY AND SECURITY

External experts serve a variety of functions in a school district, and they are funded in many different ways. Grant funds can sometimes be used to hire external experts to help districts meet grant objectives that it cannot effectively staff internally. Often, external experts hired with grant funds are uniquely qualified to advise districts on issues associated with the grant.

Many federal grants address issues that are of particular national or state interest. After Oklahoma City, Columbine and 9/11, school safety and security issues became a high national, state, and local priority. Federal grant funds can help districts address security issues. In 2008, the district was awarded the federal Readiness and Emergency Management for Schools (REMS) grant for $250,000.00. This grant is intended to assist the district in their efforts toward improving school safety and security. In the grant request for proposals, specific safety and security goals were articulated. Each district also articulated additional goals that were to be achieved over the grant period.

A critical component to the success of the grant implementation was a nationally recognized external expert, Ken Trump and his firm, National School Safety and Security Services (NSSSS). Mr. Trump's firm specializes in helping school districts implement large-scale state and federal safety grants, and provides a wide variety of safety-related services. These safety services include security and emergency preparedness assessments, traditional training sessions, and simulation drill/practice sessions.

A significant portion of the grant budget was used for Mr. Trump's services. His initial fees for services were around $115,000 dollars. Mr. Trump's work was comprehensive and resulted in successfully meeting grant objectives, and in implementing several items that were not part of the original grant, but improved district safety to a significant degree.

Mr. Trump's firm provided a full range of services to the district over the 18-month period of the grant implementation. First, Mr. Trump conducted security and emergency preparedness assessments of the schools, including charter schools and local parochial schools. These assessments included site visits to the buildings, analyzing potential hazards, and meeting with administrative staff to determine their concerns with safety.

These security and emergency preparedness assessments were conducted in the district schools, and were also conducted in the day care centers that partnered with the district to provide the four-year-old kindergarten program. Many of these day care centers were operated out of homes or small commercial buildings, and they did not have secured entrances or formal check in procedures for parents and guests. When a police matter occurred near one of these day care centers, the day care providers were not notified of the incident like the public schools were. In short, the work of Mr. Trump helped the school district work more closely with the partner day care facilities to coordinate with police and other first responders.

Mr. Trump also provided virtually all of the training required as part of the grant implementation. This training complied with the federal grant requirements, and used the latest protocol for emergency management planning. The training included the four-phase framework used at state and national levels for emergency management planning (mitigation, preparedness, response, recovery) and the protocols for incident management in case of an incident requiring emergency response. The framework and protocols learned were very practical and broadened the scope of emergency planning so that it was useful in many school contexts, including hosting large-scale events and managing small-scale, in-school disturbances.

Finally, Mr. Trump provided additional drill and practice for building emergency response teams. Several teams met in training and simulations, and over the course of several hours, a crisis unfolded from relatively small, easy-to-manage events to a major event with national implications. Teams worked together to determine how they would manage each step and what tasks each team member would perform. Members of the local police department and school resource officers were also present during the simulation.

In order to accommodate all of these training sessions for all stakeholders, Mr. Trump made several visits, each lasting two to three days. Trainings and simulations were large-scale undertakings, and included sessions for parents, volunteers, secretarial staff, support staff, and the media. Local private and parochial schools were included whenever possible. All trainings and simulations were held during the school day, and each session was held multiple times to accommodate staff absences from their schools.

In addition to all of the training sessions and drills Mr. Trump's firm provided, he also outlined next steps and conducted follow up so that the district was clear on how to practically apply the learning from the trainings and simulations. School-level trainings, an increased number and variety of school safety drills, and rewritten school level and district level crisis plans were part of this follow up. Mr. Trump also fully understood the grant reporting/accountability piece for the federal government and was always making note of items that the district should remember to include in their grant reporting. Textbox 4.3 recalls Ms. Van Deuren's experience shadowing Mr. Trump during security and emergency preparedness assessments and meetings with stakeholders.

A motivated internal team was available to fully administer the grant. The superintendent was required to sign off on all of the grant activities, and provided the final oversight. The student services director served as the grant director, and a new district position was created to fill the need for a project manager. Both the grant director and project manager were involved in writing the REMS grant. No extra money was paid to full-time district employees serving on the internal grant implementation team, although the project manager (a part-time grant writer) was paid a stipend of approximately $24,000 dollars. In addition, Ms. Van Deuren served as the external grant evaluator and was paid a stipend of approximately $10,000 dollars. Other internal staff time was allocated to the grant implementation, although these allocations were limited, primarily due to employees' regular workloads.

Box 4.3   Shadowing An Expert

As Ms. Van Deuren recalls:

There are many interesting things to learn by shadowing a national consultant. After my service on the board and in my role as grant evaluator, I was part of the district grant team that shadowed Mr. Trump and his associate as he conducted security and emergency preparedness assessments and meetings with day care providers and principals. These experiences provided our team with the opportunity to have Mr. Trump share his observations, as well as observing ways he facilitated meetings to learn about the concerns of those individuals who worked on the sites. Having direct involvement in this part of the grant implementation provided our grant team with insight on how to achieve the goals of the grant more effectively, and also how to implement additional measures (often at low or no cost) that would have a significant positive impact on the safety of the schools and partner facilities in the district.

First, our team accompanied Mr. Trump on several building security and emergency preparedness assessments. While Mr. Trump conducted these assessments throughout the district, on this particular day, the assessments were conducted in the district's charter school buildings. The buildings that house the charter schools are, for the most part, non-traditional school facilities that the district leases. In addition, most of the charter schools serve an at-risk student population. As such, most of these facilities present unique challenges in terms of building hazards and student safety.

The purpose of the security and emergency preparedness assessments was to ascertain from a physical standpoint the hazards unique to each building. Mr. Trump went through each building systematically, observing a number of things that could be deemed hazardous. These items included entrances without security systems (buzzers or cameras), "blind" entrances where school personnel could not see who was coming in or out until the door was opened, and site lines from buildings to walkways and parking lots. During these assessments, Mr. Trump and his associate talked our team through his observations and encouraged questions and comments from the grant team. Some of the items that Mr. Trump identified were in the process of being addressed by the district, while many others were not. Detailed notes were made on all items, and as a result of the assessments, many newly identified items were also addressed.

While Mr. Trump was conducting these assessments, it was interesting to note that many of the changes that he recommended were low- or no-cost fixes. For example, by moving desk positions in one charter school, students were more strategically placed away from the main entrance and would not have their backs to the door. Moving a large desk for an adult to sit near the front entrance would offer additional security. Locking a door to a staircase leading to an unused second floor would prevent students from going to that second floor when they had no business being there.

Second, our team attended meetings with building leaders to learn about the specific safety concerns they had in each building. Meetings were also held with day care facility providers who were in the first year of partnering with the district to offer a district-sponsored 4-year-old kindergarten program. Mr. Trump facilitated each of these meetings, and each group brought forth different concerns. The concerns brought forth by the day care facility providers were particularly insightful and interesting. For example, the day care providers wanted to know more about the best ways to handle upset or irate parents. They were also concerned about the lack of notification by the police when a police incident was unfolding near the facilities. The school district would be called when an incident was occurring near one of the schools, but not when an incident was occurring near a district day care partner. As a result of these conversations, several day care facilities took proactive steps to improve their security and protocols, were put in place to notify day care facilities of police incidents occurring in the area.

Mr. Trump helped the district coordinate first responders, secondary responders (e.g., the Red Cross), partner day care facilities, private schools, and parochial schools. These entities formed a district-focused community wide School Safety Council (SSC). The members of this council were strategically and regularly involved in the details of planning and executing action steps taken by the district on the school safety initiative. The SSC represented the foundation for sustaining the school's safety initiative years beyond the grant period. The result of Mr. Trump's work in the district is not only an improved emergency management plan for the district, but also improved emergency management coordination among all of the schools and first responders in the city.

An important component of Mr. Trump's work with the school district was providing guidance on ways to effectively address a variety of emergency/incident/safety-related issues with external publics. His article in the March 2009 *American School Board Journal,* Communicating Safety, summarizes many of the points that he emphasized in trainings and simulations in the district, including the following:

- "Staying out in front," which details a variety of proactive steps to ensure that preventative measures are being taken and that all personnel in the community are properly prepared in the event of an incident.
- Managing rumors and threats, which involves having a solid crisis communication plan in place, managing the vehicles through which rumors are spread (cell phones), and educating students about reporting rumors and threats to adults (proper and improper reporting).
- Response during and after a crisis, including how to provide timely updates, use multiple mechanisms for communication, and how to debrief, learn, and better prepare for future incidents.

Mr. Trump's work was very valuable to the district in several respects. He came in with specialized knowledge no one in the district possessed. He shared that knowledge and helped key project personnel organize and structure various systems (e.g., the building and district emergency response plans and the School Safety Council), and followed up his initial work with training and reinforcement. When Mr. Trump finished his work with the district, the district had the ability to carry on the work independently.

WILLIAM STRAUSS: THE DIFFERENCES BETWEEN GENERATIONS

Today's professional development trends in education are shifting away from the use of one-time external experts, about whom there has been much criticism, who come in to give a single presentation to a large group of staff (Riley, 1993; Wong, 2002; Cogrer, 2009; Cooper, 2009). These experts are often considered too expensive and, while they may offer valuable information, their presentations are often thought to have little lasting impact. However, there are some instances where an external expert can give a one-time presentation that offers valuable insights to help teachers, staff, and/or administrators better understand and address a particular issue.

The superintendent had the opportunity to hear William Strauss at a state conference for superintendents in May, 2005. Mr. Strauss was a specialist in generational history, and served as a lecturer and consultant to numerous public and private organizations. He was a graduate of Harvard (1969), Harvard Law School (1973), and the Kennedy School of Government (1973). Mr. Strauss was also the co-founder of the Washington, D.C.-based musical group, The Capitol Steps that specialized in satirical political comedy. As an avid supporter of the arts, Mr. Strauss encouraged educators to become more involved in serving student groups in the arts, most notably by starting the

Cappies, a critics and awards program for high school theatre students. His presentation at the superintendents' conference was titled "The Millennial Generation: Implications for School Leaders." As Dr. Evert recalls:

> Mr. Strauss was an excellent and engaging speaker. I was astounded with the global and practical aspects of his presentation and immediately thought of ways that this information could benefit the staff in our district. For several years, I had been hearing from older staff (Boomer Generation) about difficulties in connecting with younger, Generation X parents. I thought that increasing awareness of these generational differences and facilitating better understanding among all administrators of both generations could pay lasting dividends. I wanted Mr. Strauss to give his presentation to our district administrative team, and I contacted him and arranged for him to be the keynote speaker at our administrative team staff meeting in August of 2005. In addition to the administrative team and board members, administrators from surrounding districts, legislators, local chamber of commerce staff, and the media were invited to attend.

After hearing the presentation, the superintendent realized that the match between the message Mr. Strauss delivered and the questions and concerns that his administrators were voicing was perfect. He decided to invite Mr. Strauss to address district administrators with the talk that he gave at the superintendents' conference. The fees for this engagement ran approximately $5,000.00 plus expenses, which the superintendent covered out of his discretionary budget. The board was informed of this expenditure (and, of course, encouraged to participate in the presentation), but no formal approval was sought.

Administrative staff and several board members from approximately 10 surrounding districts attended Mr. Strauss's presentation in August of 2005. He arrived the evening before the scheduled date of the presentation, and was able to visit for some time with the superintendent to get an idea of the questions and concerns being raised among administrators. Mr. Strauss also toured the community. He was very interested in the history and demographics of the community and the district. Spending this additional time working with the superintendent and/or other key stakeholders is common for external experts so that they can deliver what they have to offer in the most effective manner possible.

The focus of the presentation was to share his research, which shows that very real differences exist between the generations. He focused on Generation X parents, Millennial Generation students, and Generation X staff. Mr. Strauss defined specific characteristics of several generations, including the Missionary Generation (born 1860–1882), the Lost Generation (born 1883–1890), the GI Generation (born 1901–1924), the Silent Generation (born 1925–1942), the Boomer Generation (born 1943–1960), Generation X (born 1961–1981), and the Millennial Generation (born 1982–2002).

Mr. Strauss delivered several very important messages relevant to Boomer Generation administrators, Generation X parents, and Millennial Generation students. The messages to Boomer Generation administrators focused on the ways that they could work more effectively with Generation X parents. It was suggested that Boomer Generation administrators work through their own grief cycle of leaving behind lower accountability systems and learn to accept and work within the new framework of accountability and standardized testing inherent in the No Child Left Behind Act (NCLB). As Mr. Strauss said, "There's no turning back. So get over it. Deal with it. Teach the core knowledge. That's what Boomers are associated with. Be the exemplars. Be middle-aged and old. Don't try to be the young generation."

There is also need for Boomer Generation administrators to be seen by Generation X parents as student advocates, particularly in the area of co-curricular activities. Without strong co-curricular activities, Generation X parents are more likely to send their children to private schools or choose home schooling as alternatives to a public school education. Boomer Generation administrators may also consider being more transparent, describe student assessment measures in greater detail, and create media opportunities that share the good stories of students.

According to Mr. Strauss, Generation X parents are searching for specific qualities in their schools, including transparency, accountability, and reality over ideology. Generation X parents are very different from Boomer Generation parents, having been raised in a climate of negativity about public education. That is, these parents heard over and over how public schools were failing. Generation X parents are more challenging of public education, and question the degree of funding public schools need. Generation X parents are already saturated by bad news about schools, so there is no positive benefit to using bad news in an attempt to create urgency to action among these parents. In the eyes of Generation X parents, administrators would do well by easing time constraints on students and reducing stress and anxiety over grades.

Mr. Strauss's messages about Millennial students focused on the fact that Millennial students are serious about school and overall doing well academically, although they face real and unique challenges in today's educational setting. Mr. Strauss described several positive characteristics and circumstances of the current high school student population, including:

- a rise in alternatives to traditional education,
- a decline in crime and substance abuse,
- an increase in positive peer pressure,
- an increase in the number of high achieving girls to record levels,
- a high level of knowledge about and comfortable with technology, and
- a high level of participation in extracurricular activities.

Mr. Strauss also described several unique challenges, issues, and characteristics that Millennial students were facing, including:

- a high stress level over homework, grades, and college admission,
- a decline in physical activity,
- a large amount of instructional time spent learning how to take tests, which may inhibit creativity,
- a higher participation rate in gangs among minority males, particularly Latino and Asian males, and
- an increase in the number of issues with sleep and eating disorders.

Textbox 4.4 contains the superintendent's recollections about why he decided to have Mr. Strauss speak in the district, including the issues that principals were identifying and the ways the Mr. Strauss addressed those

---

Box 4.4   Making The Most Of A One-Time Expert

Dr. Evert recalls:
During the 2005 State Superintendents' conference, I heard Mr. Strauss speak about generational differences. My administrators had expressed concerns about dealing with the current generation of parents. They indicated that there was a communication gap between themselves as Boomer Generation administrators and Generation X parents. I heard Mr. Strauss clearly and effectively address the questions and issues that the administrators were asking. I believed he accurately articulated the dynamic between the two generations and offered strategies and approaches that would be helpful to my administrators. I wanted to invite him to our district to address our administrative team.

As his presentation continued, Mr. Strauss indicated that key decision-making positions, such as legislative seats and board of education seats were being filled more and more with Generation X individuals. This new generation of decision makers was different than previous generations and often required a different approach to interaction. As he spoke, I thought more about bringing Mr. Strauss in to speak to our administrators and thought it might be a good idea to expand the audience to reach more of the people with whom the district interacted on funding, policy-making, and other related issues. I believed that a better understanding of generational issues and knowledge of a common vocabulary of terminology would enable us to move forward more effectively on certain issues.

> Invitations were extended to all district administrative team members, district board members, and administrators from approximately 10 other local districts. In addition, invitations were also extended to area legislators, Cooperative Education Service Agency (CESA) administrators, area superintendents, local chamber of commerce staff, local community college administrators, local technical college administrators, and the local media. In total, approximately 150 were in attendance. The event was held at the technical college in order to showcase the strong partnership between the school district and the local area colleges.

issues. Bringing in a one-time external expert was not a regular occurrence in the district, but the superintendent believed that Mr. Strauss would provide some of the help and answers that administrators were seeking regarding their interactions with parents and students with different generational characteristics from their own.

Administrative team members at the presentation found the information very helpful, especially when dealing with Generation X parents, Generation X staff members, and Millennial students. Because all of the administrative team attended the presentation, they all had a similar framework and vocabulary to discuss the implications of generations in their schools and classrooms. The superintendent was able to refer regularly and repeatedly to Mr. Strauss's work in various contexts, with the knowledge that the administrative team and board members would understand the meaning of the references.

The education reporter from the local newspaper also attended the presentation. As a result, two in-depth follow-up articles appeared in the paper. The unusually extensive coverage provided the entire community with a detailed overview of Mr. Strauss's presentation. This extensive coverage reflected very positively on the school district and significantly increased Mr. Strauss's impact and the positive benefits of the presentation to the school district.

The information given by Mr. Strauss in his presentation did not require a great deal of formal follow up or implementation; rather, it was intended to create awareness and provide a framework for helping administrators recognize that generational differences and perspectives are real and that they do impact what happens in the schools. That being said, Mr. Strauss did offer several suggestions for follow up, and many administrators were highly motivated by Mr. Strauss's presentation and did their own follow up by reading, studying, and discussing additional sources on the subject of generational differences. In addition, Mr. Strauss granted the district permission to use his power-point presentation after his visit.

Often, (typically in an effort to save money) districts send a handful of people to a conference or presentation and ask them to report to the rest of the organization upon their return. This approach works for some types of information and contexts. There are occasions when the message and the messenger are powerful enough to merit the effort to bring them into the district so that a large audience can benefit from the full experience. Mr. Strauss's information was comprehensive, detailed, and well organized. Most importantly, the message was delivered with great impact.

The superintendent was sufficiently impacted by Mr. Strauss and his message during the May 2005 superintendents' conference that he strongly believed the district would benefit from inviting Mr. Strauss to the district, even if it was only for one presentation. While the use of one-time external experts may not be popular in current professional development trends, they can serve a beneficial purpose if used strategically and in an appropriate context. It is also much more efficient and cost effective to bring in an external expert to talk to a large group than it is to send numerous staff members to conferences.

Textbox 4.5 highlights the benefits and insights that Mr. Strauss provided to the superintendent. As a result of Mr. Strauss's visit and the opportunity

---

Box 4.5 Maximizing Professional Development Opportunities for District Leaders

Dr. Evert recalls:

I was most impressed by Mr. Strauss and his message. As a result of his presentation (which I had the privilege of hearing twice) and being able to visit with him, generational differences became something that I paid a great deal of attention to over the next several years. Mr. Strauss and his co-author Neil Howe were prolific writers, and I read many of their books to better understand the nuances of generational differences. In addition I found helpful articles, several from *The School Administrator* that were also relevant (*See* References). Reading is a critical part of my own commitment to stay current and improve my leadership. I read professional periodicals, several local and state newspapers on a daily basis, and other publications that I can find which seem to have relevance to issues and items that are part of whatever professional role I am undertaking. I keep a personal bibliography of materials that I find relevant and useful, and during my tenure as superintendent I shared much of this information with board members, directors, and other stakeholders.

to speak with him at some length, the superintendent was made aware of an important nuance in human relations (generational differences) that helped to be a better district leader and to facilitate the type of coalition-building that effectively moved the district forward.

LESSONS LEARNED

Each of the three experts discussed in this chapter provided a high level of service to the district in their respective capacities. They were each very knowledgeable, highly qualified, and were selected based on their ability and recommendations. Each was hired to fill a highly specialized role in the district with the similarity that each specialized role was limited in time and/or scope. That is, all of the issues that the experts were hired to address needed a high level of knowledge and expertise for which the district did not need a full-time and/or long-term employee.

Unique lessons were learned from each expert:

- The most important lesson learned from Ms. Wirth was the importance of having confidence and trust in the expertise and objectivity of a financial expert. The knowledge and objectivity Ms. Wirth brought to the table on sensitive financial issues helped the board and administration move forward more efficiently and effectively on those issues.
- Mr. Trump's time in the district illustrated the advantages of seeking federal funds to help the district address comprehensive issues, such as district-wide safety and security. Mr. Trump was very knowledgeable about the ways that these federal grants were typically imple.mented and assessed, and as a result, he made the administrative process much smoother than it would have been without him. The district also learned new things about hiring and staffing for a large-scale federal grant through working with Mr. Trump.
- Engaging Mr. Strauss to address an ongoing concern that had been voiced in the district reinforced the importance of listening to administrators and staff about their professional development needs. As part of his presentation, Mr. Strauss provided a great deal of written materials that the district was able to use in many different ways over a long period of time as effective follow up.

Perhaps the most important lesson learned from all of these experts is how important it is to hire individuals with the same degree of quality and care as any other position that is hired in the district. The purpose of hiring these experts is to address an issue that internal resources do not have the time and/or specialization to address. Quality individuals who deliver quality services are essential to achieving the goals for which they were hired. Each of these external experts arrived at the district through very different means, but upon reflection, there is no question that each was precisely the right match for the tasks at hand.

One other important lesson that was learned from these external experts is that creative funding solutions can yield great benefits to school districts. Each external expert was compensated through alternative funding options, including grants, discretionary funds, and commissions. A high level of trust between the board and administration enabled the administration to effectively and efficiently hire these specialists as excellent targeted change agents.

External experts can be effective in many areas of district leadership and management, including operations. They are especially helpful when specialized knowledge is required that is not reasonable to expect that district personnel possess. They can also be an excellent resource when there is a short-term or occasional need that requires expertise but does not justify or fit the guidelines for hiring a full- or part-time employee.

External experts can be very effective at assisting the district with special projects, including grant implementations and referendum service. These projects typically require efforts above and beyond the normal business of the district and they are critically important to district growth and development. Special projects like those mentioned in this chapter often involve large sums of money, and it is imperative that the individuals involved in seeing them through to completion are highly qualified to ensure that all aspects of implementation are handled correctly.

One context in which external experts have received criticism as a group is when they are engaged to give one-time presentations in a district. However, depending on the subject matter and the district context, occasional one-time presenters can be very effective. Even though a one-time presenter is, by definition, only available to district personnel for one visit, an effective presenter will typically want some background of the district and perhaps want to spend some one-on-one time with district leaders to maximize the impact of the visit. They may also be willing to leave ample information and resources with the district to enable district personnel to engage in follow up.

Chapter 5

Transferring and Implementing Proven Health Care Leadership Concepts to Public Education

Many changes occurred in the district during the superintendent's first decade of service. Dr. Golarz facilitated change in the district decision-making model, and as a result, the mission, vision, and long-range plan (updated in 1995, 2000, and 2005) were more clearly articulated and aligned with the activities in the district. Dr. Odom had provided guidance with issues related to the changing demographics in the community and the achievement gap between white and minority students.

The business director, with the help of Carol Wirth, had done an excellent job of maintaining the district's healthy financial status, including maintaining favorable bond ratings, a high fund balance, and accurate, detailed accounting records. In addition, the district enjoyed a high level of support from students, parents, and the community under strong, student-centered board leadership. All things considered, the district was running smoothly. The superintendent had discovered through experience that Dr. Jerry Patterson (1993) was right: Lasting change takes about 7–10 years to accomplish.

At the ten-year mark, the questions became: What next? What were the best ways to facilitate a new wave of change? How does a superintendent avoid becoming stale by guarding the status quo? How does a long-term leader instill a renewed sense of urgency among staff and community? How does a long-term leader keep an organization fresh and moving forward in the wake of new challenges, like No Child Left Behind (NCLB), continuing changes in community demographics, and unprecedented, continuous budget reductions?

In addition to the using resources available through state and national organizations for school leaders, the superintendent continued to study and search for ideas from a variety of sources, including Adelman and Taylor (2006), Elmore (2007), Dufour (2007), and Studer (2003, 2005). He continued to search for new ways to move the district forward and to address new and existing problems and issues.

Dr. Evert recalls:

During the 2005–06 school year, my thoughts turned to what I might do as superintendent to create a greater sense of urgency in the district. I believed we should continue to increase student achievement and strive for greater staff involvement and ownership of our district. Having completed ten years as superintendent, I enjoyed the good fortune of working for and with excellent board members. I was beginning to reflect on my career and look at the possibility of my retirement sometime within the next three years or so.

Even though we as a district accomplished many great things for students over the past ten years, things were not perfect, and many things were not where I believed they should be. Chronic problems included addressing the learning needs of a student population which had tripled in the number of students considered at or below the poverty level, very difficult and contentious labor relations surrounding collective bargaining with our 800-plus members teacher union, and the need for several million dollars of budget reductions each year as a result of less state aid.

Returning to the sense of urgency and an impending retirement, it was difficult for me to quantify what I meant by urgency. I did reduce my thoughts to writing in a fall 2005 memo to the board. The focus of the memo was on my belief that we as a district needed to avoid complacency and to address several ongoing issues. These issues were centered around becoming more responsive to consumer concerns (especially parents), becoming more sensitive to diversity issues, and increasing our efforts to improve achievement levels for all students, especially those in poverty. The board gave me very positive feedback on correctly identifying the most pressing issues in our district.

Around this time, I read two of Quint Studer's books regarding leadership in the field of health care, *Hardwiring Excellence: Purpose, Worthwhile Work, Making a Difference* (2003) and *101 Answers to Questions Leaders Ask* (2005). These books focused on the need for high energy, results-driven leadership. Mr. Studer's work was especially interesting to me because I knew him personally, and we had worked together on various projects in the late 1970s and early 1980s. Mr. Studer was a district special education teacher before I met him. He left education in the mid-1980s and went into health care administration, including serving as CEO of a hospital. Mr. Studer left hospital administration to start his own consulting firm, Studer Group, which has been highly successful in helping hospitals provide better service to patients and a better work environment for staff.

FROM IDEAS TO ACTION

In the summer of 2007, a unique opportunity was presented to the district as the result of a chance meeting. The superintendent and Mr. Studer met at the funeral of a former teacher and father of a board member. As they talked, both expressed an interest in exploring whether or not Studer's proven, results-oriented leadership program would work in a public school setting.

As a result of this and subsequent discussions, the superintendent attended a two-day Studer Group training session in Tennessee during the fall of 2007 that provided an overview of the entire program. The Studer Group waived the conference fee for attendance, and the superintendent paid for his own travel, lodging, and expenses. During this conference, the superintendent and Mr. Studer had opportunities to talk. As former colleagues often do when they have not seen each other for many years, there was a free-flowing exchange of ideas, which included the potential for personal and professional partnerships. The superintendent and Mr. Studer began to consider whether part or all of the initiative might be effective in a public school setting, and whether the school district would be a good candidate for attempting an implementation.

In mid-December 2007, a group of 12 school district board members, administrators, and teacher union leaders attended the same two-day training session in Florida that the superintendent had attended in Tennessee a few months earlier. On the morning after the conference, representatives from the Escambia County School District and Mr. Studer spoke to the district group. The Escambia County School District had implemented several Studer Group techniques in their schools. The district group returned from the training excited and enthusiastic about the possibilities for positive change the Studer Group approach might bring to the district. Over the next several weeks, board members, administrators, and teacher union leaders spoke to leaders from several other districts that had used at least some of the Studer Group concepts in their districts. In addition, Mr. Studer visited the district to answer questions and address representative district staff and all board members before the board formally adopted the initiative.

Mr. Studer formally offered to partner with the district and fund the initiative for a period of three years if the district would agree to serve as a "lab" or "demonstration" district. The contract drawn by Studer group and approved by the board reads that "[t]he professional fee and term of engagement for the above with an organization comparable in size to . . . [the district] would be $400 thousand per year for each of 3 years, or $1.2 million." The formal contract containing this language was presented to the board and was accepted by a 9–0 vote in January of 2008.

Although the Studer Group covered most of the costs of the initiative, it is important to note that the partnership between the Studer Group and the school district has not been cost free for the district, nor was it intended to be. In June, 2010, the local paper reported that over the 2.5 year period that the contract had been in place, the district spent approximately $80,000, mostly on transportation, lodging, and other customary expenses associated with sending district personnel to Studer Group seminars.

Studer Group paid the seminar fees and flight costs for all approved district attendees, and the district covered other expenses. The funding for these expenses was allocated from one or more of the following sources: (1) approximately $20,000 that the board approved in the 2008–2009 budget for Studer Group expenses; (2) a district-wide staff development budget overseen by the director of curriculum and instruction; (3) central office department budgets overseen by directors and coordinators; and (4) school professional development budgets overseen by school principals.

The partnership between the Studer Group and the district was an exciting and unique opportunity. Dr. Evert recalls:

> The compelling factor that lead me to endorse the partnership was my belief that by looking at new leadership concepts and techniques, we might ignite our district and propel it past the current level of unrest (and comfort!) to a new level of urgency. Mr. Studer described his program as a "fire starter" effort. I was intrigued and convinced that the journey itself would lead to improvement. Mr. Studer's approach also appealed to me because it would provide both formal and informal opportunities for others in the district to expand their leadership roles and demonstrate their capabilities. Heath (2009) describes this approach as "leading from the back."

By partnering with the Studer Group, the district intended to make significant district-wide improvements in several areas, including the following:

- Improve leadership at the district and school levels by reducing leadership variance
- Focus leadership on evidence and results
- Involve representative staff in the development of standards of excellence
- Measure improvement effectively
- Apply proven/successful health care techniques ("prescriptive 'to dos;'") to the school district
- Involve parents and students at a higher level in the form of more feedback and communication
- Unite all in our community's efforts to provide a world-class education for each student

ASSESSING IMPLEMENTATION USING A SYSTEM FLAWS FRAMEWORK

Jenkins (2008) discusses several underlying problems with today's education system. He identifies these underlying problems as system flaws. According to Jenkins, these system flaws prevent today's education system from producing much more than it currently does, and in order to realize significant and lasting changes in education, the system flaws must be addressed.

Seven system flaws are identified by Jenkins: (1) teachers spend too much time reteaching; (2) students are accountable for short-term memory, but schools are accountable for students' long-term memory; (3) school use inappropriate measurement tools to define success in a manner applicable to as many students as possible; (4) schools add programs but do not add time; therefore, subtraction is not organized; (5) schools rarely collect baseline data; (6) there is disagreement between teachers and administrators over the role of homework; and (7) key concepts are not aligned throughout the educational organization. Jenkins also acknowledges ". . . education needs new approaches to address the systemic issues" (p. 38).

The discussions between Mr. Studer and the superintendent resulted in a proposal that Studer Group implement practices and protocols throughout the district designed to create organizational change that would address several of the system flaws identified by Jenkins. Specifically, the Studer Group systemically and proactively addressed issues related to developing and using objective measurement tools, gathering and using baseline data, adding new programs/discontinuing ineffective programs, and aligning key concepts (Studer, 2008). By using prescriptive techniques and insisting on certain "must haves," the Studer Group worked to realign the purpose, mission, and vision of an organization.

Jenkins identifies inappropriate measures as a problem with current school systems. Studer Group endorses the use of objective measurement tools for school leaders. Using Studer Group's objective measurement tools has helped the district establish goals from the board/superintendent level, and set specific, measurable achievements for each goal identified. Eventually, these goals should cascade throughout the district to the teacher and staff levels. These goals and outcomes are set and assigned a weight or value for each administrative leader and became the criteria for each administrator's individualized evaluation. Identifying specific, measurable outcomes in the goal-setting process created a new urgency among district leaders to focus on those goals that were assigned the most weight or value in the goal-setting process.

Jenkins states that schools rarely collect baseline data. Baseline data are a critical component of Studer Group's plan for schools. Baseline data are directly linked to administrative leadership evaluations, and are used to set objective, measurable goals for desired outcomes. Studer Group asked the district to draw on readily available district information for their baseline data, including attendance rates, truancy rates, graduation rates, test scores, grade point averages, and fiscal data. In addition, the perceptions of parents and staff were determined using survey techniques, which provided useful data, both for baseline and follow up.

Jenkins indicates that schools too often add programs and engage in "disorganized subtraction" to remove programs. Another important concept that Studer Group advocates is to keep and systematize what works best (best practices) and eliminate programs and practices that do not work well. One specific technique the district uses to systematize best practices and to discover ineffective and inefficient practices is borrowed directly from hospitals called "rounding." The term is derived from rounds doctors make regularly on patients to assess patient progress.

Simply put, rounding is a technique that school leaders use to assess teacher satisfaction. Rounding provides opportunities for individuals in supervisory positions to check in with those whom they supervise for directed, purposeful, and constructive feedback. Rounding is different than "walk-throughs" (Downey, 2004) and other evaluation techniques, in that rounding focuses on principal, school, and district improvement through open dialogue and without evaluating the teacher's performance, whereas walk-throughs and other evaluation techniques focus on teacher improvement and accountability.

Rounding and other techniques used by the Studer Group provided several opportunities for staff members to incorporate these concepts into their own professional development, including dissertations and white papers. Textbox 5.1 highlights some of the work done by district staff based on the Studer Group technique of rounding.

Finally, Jenkins indicates that too often, key concepts are not aligned throughout the organization. Creating the alignment that Jenkins describes is at the core of all Studer Group concepts. Proper alignment addresses fundamental issues of purpose and enables the district to focus on strategic plans and goals in meaningful and purposeful ways. This alignment begins with organizational tools.

Every function of the school district can be described as belonging to one of five or six broad categories or "Pillars." These pillars enable the district to track ways in which all actions and implementations affect the district as a whole. In addition, organizing the district by pillars enables all stakeholders to better understand how their departments and job descriptions fit into the larger objective of educating children.

Alignment continues with leadership evaluations, which align the mission, vision, and purpose of the district with its daily operations and decision-making. Several other practices and protocols have been implemented that

Box 5.1 Staff Development Opportunities

The partnership between the Studer Group and the school district has affected the district in many ways, including the creation of opportunities for staff development and adult learning. Several staff members, administrators, and central office staff went beyond merely implementing the program to studying and reflecting on the ways it was affecting the district. Two examples are cited in this section.

In the first example, a high school assistant principal used the rounding technique as the basis for his doctoral dissertation, studying the effects of rounding on principal leadership and school climate (Keyser, 2010). The study included two middle schools and one high school, each with no turnover in principal leadership during course of the study. Staff members (with no turnover during the course of the study) rated these principals (using a pre-test, post-test model) in the spring of 2008 and the winter of 2009. The principals rounded on each staff member at least once between the first and second surveys. The results were clear. Specifically, Dr. Keyser reported "results [which] indicated that teachers believed the principal's leadership was enhanced due to the process of rounding for outcomes, as well as the feeling that the school climate had improved."

In the second example, two middle school principals accepted the superintendent's invitation to write a white paper on how rounding for outcomes was different from administrative "walk-throughs." The summary presented in Ehrhardt and Sperry's paper entitled *Rounding Versus Walk-Through Supervision* (2009) provides a review of the similarities and differences between rounding and walk-throughs from a principal's perspective. The similarities and differences identifies by Ehrhardt and Sperry are as follows:

Similarities

- Facilitate the principal's knowledge of what is working/not working in a school
- Potential to improve school climate
- Need to be scheduled as part of a principal's routine duties
- Enhance the sense of staff ownership in the school
- Improve job satisfaction and student achievement

Differences

- Each activity generates a different data set and objectives
- Rounding has the objective of gathering staff opinions regarding specific areas
- Walk-throughs generate specific observations used to improve teacher performance

align and clarify expectations for performance, behavior, and results. This alignment is designed to create a more effective and efficient school district with a high level of consistency among and within schools.

IMPLEMENTATION AND PROGRESS

As part of the implementation process, the superintendent communicated on a regular basis with the board regarding development and progress of the partnership with Studer Group for over a year and a half before his retirement. For example, a memo to board members in early January, 2009 (approximately one year after the approval of the contract with Studer Group) highlighted four areas of implementation on the initiative. These activities included:

1. *Rounding.* Administrators underwent specialized training on rounding, because it was so different than other evaluation techniques, both in what it was intended to evaluate and how it was administered.
2. *Extensive training for administrative team members (school leaders).* Called the Leadership Development Institute, these in-depth training sessions included several training objectives. Studer Group staff and central office staff led and participated in these trainings, and the sessions were held in addition to regularly scheduled trainings on other district related topics.
3. *Report of monthly meetings with the internal Studer Group steering committee.* A steering committee comprised of the superintendent, board members, central office staff, building leaders, teachers, and parent representatives met monthly to discuss the progress of the implementation of the Studer Group program and to plan and organize next steps. These meetings were very helpful in gauging the perceptions of various stakeholders regarding the program and assessing what was working well and what was not. Detailed minutes of these meetings were taken and distributed to the board and administrative team.
4. *Central office staff meetings.* Central office staff received regular briefings regarding Studer Group activities in the district. In December 2008, three central office committees were formed to address concerns of central office employees, including physical climate, inter-office communication, and the specific mission of the central office.

The superintendent worked on the Studer Group initiative from fall of 2007 until February of 2009. In many respects, the initiative was progressing well;

however, at the same time, there was considerable tension that had developed between the board and superintendent regarding several district issues, which included problems with district technology services, contract issues regarding snow days and making up class time, budget development for 2009–2010, a new round of teacher negotiations, the need to develop a new five-year long-range plan, and the need to fill upcoming administrative vacancies, mostly due to retirements.

Addressing many difficult issues in the district and the undertaking of a new major initiative took its toll on the board and superintendent. In addition, the superintendent had announced his retirement in October 2008, effective June 2009. The impending change in leadership placed additional pressure on the board. As a result the superintendent and the board agreed to the superintendent's earlier retirement, which took effect as of February 10, 2009.

The efforts of the Studer Group and the district in partnership continue. Mr. Studer recognized the possibility that his work in health care might be beneficial in an education setting. He was interested in implementing these ideas in his hometown, where the size, and demographics were favorable for the pilot. The partnership with Studer Group also illustrates the results that can be achieved when a board and superintendent are willing to take risks and venture beyond traditional leadership methods in education. Today, the district defines the partnership with Studer Group as a "Journey to Excellence," and it is important for district leaders to monitor where and how this journey will be successful and transferrable to other districts.

LESSONS LEARNED

The Studer Group/district partnership created a new level of awareness and excitement, in the district, as well as some apprehension. It can be safely stated that a number of lessons were learned from this unique health care/education venture. Each of the six lessons identified in this section involve one or more of the following general components: (1) the need for clear communication, (2) the need to establish the delegation of responsibilities for various aspects of decision-making and implementation, and (3) the importance of establishing clear goals that define success for the effort.

Arguably, the most important lesson learned from working with the Studer Group is that there is a significant difference between working with an external expert who is paid for their services and one who is donating their services. The board, district personnel, and the community were very appreciative of the generous gift given by the Studer Group. As a result, administrators seemed less inclined than they might normally have been to challenge, question, or veto any parts of the initiative that they did not understand or with which they did not entirely agree.

In effect, the donation of services by the Studer Group created a different balance of power and influence than had existed with other external experts. With other external experts, the superintendent would exercise decision-making authority, and/or delegate that authority. The board would typically have little involvement in most initiatives that they formally approved during the implementation phase. The Studer Group initiative was markedly different in that the board was very involved throughout the implementation phase.

The concern with donated services was that it appeared to disrupt the usual system of checks and balances regarding decision-making. The district was so appreciative of the donated gift, that the board and superintendent marginalized the fact that the external expert took a stronger leadership role in this initiative than other external experts had taken when working with the district. The combination of the donated gift, and the district-wide, comprehensive nature of the initiative (including the focus on leadership accountability) led the board, some administrators, and the superintendent to allow the external expert to exert more authority and influence than he might otherwise have been afforded.

The second lesson learned involves the most notable unintended collateral effect of the Studer Group/district partnership. Undertaking a major partnership where both partners are highly invested, with each serving the other in unique ways can affect the fundamental channels of communication and information flow that had been in place for many years. That is, the partnership with the Studer Group changed the long-standing channels of communication that controlled the flow of information from the board to the superintendent, from the superintendent to staff, and from the superintendent to the external expert.

As result of these changes in communication flow, heightened levels of anxiety, uncertainty, and discomfort were created in the district that arguably hindered the smooth transfer and implementation of some Studer Group concepts from a health care setting to an education setting. In hindsight, the superintendent could have addressed these changes in the channels of communication and flow of information as soon as they started to occur. Then communication channels and information flow in the Studer Group/district partnership context and other district operational contexts would have been compatible.

The third important lesson learned is that embarking on a partnership where the external expert donates services may mean that the desired final outcomes for each partner may be quite different. For example, in the district partnership with the Studer Group, the district's desired final outcomes were to improve the quality of school and district leadership and to improve student achievement. The Studer Group strongly endorsed the district goals and in addition, was interested in knowing how well their health care concepts would transfer to an education setting, and whether an Education Division was a viable option for the company.

Each partner in the agreement was highly invested in the effort, and both would be greatly benefited by having positive outcomes result from the work of the partnership. In the contract agreement between the district and the Studer Group, the following clause illustrates the potential benefits that could be gained by the Studer Group as a result of this partnership:

> Materials (workbooks, tools, software, best practices, etc.) that are provided to . . . [the district] are intended for your exclusive use and are not to be shared with any other organization without the written consent of Studer Group. Studer Group may, in its discretion, share the developed intellectual capital of this engagement with other educational organizations.

The fourth important lesson learned is that boards and superintendents should carefully consider both the positive and negative ramifications of a large philanthropic donation, especially in a political context. Never had the district undergone such a significant change process under such close media and public scrutiny. This scrutiny, combined with the pressures from both partners contributed to administrative anxiety, in part because administrators were encouraged to present each phase of implementation in a positive light.

Media involvement in the partnership created even more pressure for administrators. For example, principals and district level leaders had their staff and parent satisfaction survey results published in the local paper, which created a level of public transparency to which these school leaders had never been exposed. Some viewed the transparency in a positive light. Others believed that the survey results were posted without appropriate context or an opportunity on the part of the principals to explain or improve before the results were published.

Board members and superintendents considering a partnership with an external expert, particularly one who is donating their services, should also consider the fifth lesson that was learned through the Studer Group/district partnership. It is important to understand the demands of time that such a partnership will place on existing staff and other human resources (including board members, parents, and community members).

Typically, large federal grants allow for some level of staffing to offset the extra work associated with grant implementation. This staffing may include project managers, and/or grant evaluators (*see* chapter 4, Ken Trump). Such contingencies for additional staffing did not occur in the Studer Group/district partnership, and a small group of district personnel, (most notably the superintendent's administrative assistant) ended up doing a large amount of extra work to launch the implementation efforts. In hindsight, it would have been wise for the board and superintendent to create a budget (regardless of funding source) to allow for some additional staffing while the partnership was piloting the transfer of proven techniques in health to a public school setting.

The final lesson learned is that it is acceptable on occasion to implement major changes based on a top-down decision. Although the district had a history of decision-making that involved many stakeholders and a detailed process, the unique timing of the opportunity, coupled with the superintendent's pending retirement and the board's readiness to move forward with increased leadership accountability, made the top-down decision to partner with Studer Group the right decision for the district at the right time.

The partnership with Studer Group was a top-down initiative that sometimes required a different decision-making process throughout the implementation than was established through the work of Dr. Golarz over a decade earlier. As Dufour observed in 2007, "[m]any district leaders are reluctant to champion improvement for fear of being labeled with the epithet 'top-down leader,' the unkindest cut of all" (p. 38). Even though the Superintendent's Advisory Committee (SAC) proposal process was still used and board approval sought for the initiative, many of the daily operational decisions and strategies for next steps were decided by a very small group of leaders and Mr. Studer.

Using a modified top-down approach enabled the Studer Group/district partnership to move forward quickly. The process could move quickly because it was supported by the board and superintendent, and a team of board members, administrators, and teacher leaders who were veteran staff with a clear working understanding of the district's mission and vision. These individuals attended Studer Group training before the board approved the partnership contract, and they were able to mobilize quickly to get implementation efforts underway once Board approval was obtained.

In today's economy of tight school budgets, finding new ways to work with external experts can help districts move forward with their strategic plans and long-term educational goals. As a result of embarking on a unique partnership with an external expert whose area of expertise lies in the field of health care, the district learned several important lessons about using a "non-traditional" model of engaging external experts. Boards and superintendents may want to review these lessons when considering a non-traditional partnership with an

Transferring and Implementing Proven Health Care Leadership Concepts 109

external expert designed to benefit both the district and the external expert in some manner:

- Partnering with an external expert is not the same as hiring an external expert to achieve district goals.
- Partnering with an external expert can have unintended collateral consequences, such as communication issues.
- When partnering with an external expert, the expert and the district may have different desired final outcomes.
- Partnering with an external expert as a donation or gift is likely to create significant media and public scrutiny.
- Partnering with an external expert may require additional staffing.
- A top-down decision for action may be positive and appropriate in some situations.

Chapter 6

Lessons Learned about Leadership

Serving as a school superintendent provides opportunities to address the needs of students and staff in unique ways. The superintendent affects the climate and culture of an entire district, and he or she plays the pivotal role in determining changes that often have a long-lasting and far-reaching impact on the district and the community. As has been stated several times throughout this book, superintendents should seek experience, knowledge, and counsel from a wide variety of sources, including external experts to assist them with their role as change agents.

We have used a case-study approach to examine the successful work of six external experts representing six different contexts in which an external expert may be beneficial. These experts have brought new knowledge, models, frameworks, and specialized expertise to the district, and many lessons have been learned from them. There are many specific lessons that were learned through the work of each individual expert, and these lessons are discussed in the previous chapters. In addition, another level of learning has also occurred: We have learned a great deal about the ways district leaders and external experts interact to help the district attain goals, regardless of a specific expert's specialty.

During the writing of this book, we developed a hypothesis that a relationship exists between engaging external experts successfully and the superintendent's ability to set the stage for this success. The strength of this relationship is unclear at this time. The superintendent's ability to set the stage is likely dependent on several factors, including his or her overall ability as a leader.

As part of discussing this relationship, we identified three foundational areas that made themselves evident as threads or themes throughout the research and writing process for this book. These three foundational areas are: (1) know yourself and your context; (2) develop and implement a personal agenda and a district long-range plan; (3) superintendents need professional development as much as anyone else in the district.

It is important to note that we are describing ideas, concepts, and lessons learned that were applied in an actual district environment. The positive changes in the district were achieved through the superintendent's continued development and refinement of the foundational areas discussed in this chapter. These foundational areas were identified through a great deal of reflection, discussion (sometimes heated!), review, and consideration of events occurring over a 14-year period.

Perhaps, then, what is being presented is more the "art" aspect of educational leadership and administration as opposed to the "science" of the profession. With today's emphasis on data and research consuming most aspects of leadership and administration, perhaps educational leaders lose sight of the art of leadership and its importance. Discussing, analyzing, and writing this chapter was a learning experience for us and is intended as food for thought for readers. As is appropriate to any learning endeavor, readers are encouraged to think critically and take away that which might be useful.

THREE FOUNDATIONAL AREAS FOR DISTRICT LEADERS

In analyzing, disseminating, and discussing the external experts in the previous chapters, an interesting thing happened. The discussion of external experts naturally turned to discussions about why they were hired and the superintendent's leadership style, core educational values, and approaches to leadership. In the end, it became clear that the two were inextricably linked, and a realization set in that the focus of the previous chapters was on the external experts' roles as targeted change agents and the superintendent's leadership.

Reflecting on the external experts engaged in the district over time, we were able to articulate and clarify several lessons learned about the importance of the superintendent's development as a leader. Undergoing the in depth analysis and discussion required to understand why the experts included in this book worked so well for the district resulted in three themes or threads arising over and over again. We decided to call these foundational areas of leadership, or "foundational areas." This chapter examines those foundational areas that we identified and that might be of use to current and future superintendents.

Here's what we know: When an implementation was successful in the district and the use of an external expert enhanced the outcomes and provided guidance for the process that could not have been obtained internally, the superintendent had the foundational areas in place that are discussed in this chapter. These items are not mysterious or difficult to comprehend; rather, these lessons learned (or perhaps better phrased "lessons realized") are sensible and logical, yet can be challenging to maintain, especially in an administrative position that pulls a person in many different directions at once on any given day.

The first foundational area is "know yourself and your context." A majority of school and district leaders have a variety of experiences in education before they undertake roles in district-level administration. Each role interacts differently with the strengths and weaknesses of each of us, and each role teaches us something different about ourselves and about the ways that we can best serve the students, staff, parents, community members, and others who lie within our sphere of influence. Once we begin to understand our own strengths and weaknesses, it takes a certain amount of courage and comfort with leadership to accept and embrace the knowledge of those that know more than we do (whether they are internal or external).

In addition to understanding ourselves, it is important to understand the context in which we operate, including its strengths, weaknesses, and nuances. Understanding this context enables a superintendent to identify what is working well in the district and areas that need improvement. This understanding is essential for the identification of problems and issues, and prioritization of those problems and issues, and also for identifying successes that will help the district create and maintain a positive climate and culture and balance a large amount of negativity that is likely to arise when addressing difficult issues.

The second foundational area is to develop and strive to implement an agenda and long-range plan. The agenda and plan are based on knowledge of self and context, and appropriately prioritizing problems and issues. Agendas and long-range plans are different. The agenda refers to a personal "platform" of sorts that shifts and changes little, if at all, over time.

The superintendent's agenda throughout his superintendency was to increase student learning and achievement, promote diversity and close the achievement gap, and increase parent involvement throughout the district. Agenda items are truly big picture goals and value statements for which the leader stands. Long-range plans, on the other hand, are developed with stakeholders to improve student achievement and address critical issues in the district. Lunenburg and Ornstein (1996) indicate that long-range plans are typically modified every five years or less (p. 325).

In order to effectively implement agendas and long-range plans, a critical piece of the second foundational area is to stay on task and on message. Messages should convey big ideas and include "memorable messages" and "sticky messages" (Gladwell, 2000; Marzano and Waters, 2009). These messages serve several purposes, including keeping an issue in the forefront, creating urgency to spur action, and keeping dialogue, development, planning, and action centered on the issue at hand.

The third foundational area is that superintendents need professional development as much or more than anyone else in the district. Superintendents typically have access to regional and state support systems, but those support systems are only as good as the services offered and whether a superintendent initiates participation and use of those services. Professional development for the superintendent should, over time, have a positive impact on the district to a degree proportionate to the time and money invested in it. Finding and engaging external experts, such as several of the experts discussed in this book, is one way that superintendents can acquire professional development opportunities that can benefit an entire district.

Each external expert discussed throughout this book was successful because the superintendent attended to each of these three foundational areas. It is a cumulative and interactive process. Tending to these foundational areas led to more action toward district improvement (including the involvement of external experts), and the work of the external experts pushed the superintendent to continue to grow and develop in these three foundational areas. Danielson and McGreal (2000) discuss the importance of professional development and the need for a continuous cycle of improvement. The goal is to provide all teachers, regardless of experience with ". . . a continuous cycle of assessment to ensure that all tenured teachers continue to meet the district's standards for effective teaching" (p. 100).

Developing these foundational areas and working on district improvement initiatives (with expert involvement as necessary) created a continuous cycle of learning and improvement, both for the superintendent and the district. It is the work and modeling of these experts and their positive impacts on the school district that has enabled the reflection on their experiences to lead to the lessons realized and the identification of these three foundational areas and their critical importance in aligning a district's direction and use of resources.

These general lessons are discussed from the unique combination of perspectives provided by a long-term superintendent and a new board member with an extensive education background. One thing that we learned is that no matter when a leader enters the process, they bring something of value to the work, and when they leave the process, they take away their own unique experiences and learning. As such, the reflections conveyed in this chapter illustrate the great impacts that

Know Yourself and Your Constituencies

Know Yourself

The starting point for any district leader is to know yourself. Although this statement seems oversimplified and obvious, the message entails more than might be apparent at first glance. Evans (2007) points out the importance of knowing one's self as he discusses authentic (*genuine; discovered*) leadership. "[A]uthentic leaders build their practice outward from their core commitments rather than inward from a management text" (p. 144). Evans also makes the following observations:

> A leader's philosophy remains tacit in part because none of us can be fully in touch with the entire range of our knowledge, perception, feeling, and skill. At any given moment, our reservoir of expertise is larger than we can encompass, our wellspring of inspiration deeper than we can fully tap. But it also stays hidden—even unconscious—because it is buried and discouraged by formal leadership theory taught in graduate administration courses and disseminated in leadership books (p. 144).

When self-awareness is thought of in professional terms, the concept of identifying and knowing one's own strengths and weaknesses is often the first thing that comes to mind. While knowing one's own strengths and weaknesses is important, it is only a starting point. An effective superintendent goes beyond knowing their strengths and weaknesses and has a very keen awareness of their own educational core commitments and leadership style. The core commitments drive decision-making and direction (the "what") by serving as a framework through which input from internal audiences and external publics is processed. We believe that a leader's core commitments remain relatively stable, although they may be modified or framed differently over the years as the district evolves or the context changes entirely (the leader takes a new position elsewhere).

On the other hand, leadership style determines the ways that a leader interacts with internal audiences and external publics. Various aspects of leadership style may be more or less effective and such variance can and does influence a leader's ability to obtain results based on his or her core commitments and values. Leadership style also affects the leader's approach to action steps (the "how"). How the leader sets the agenda and direction, the degree to which a leader delegates responsibilities, the timelines for completion of tasks, and the assessments used to determine the success of an undertaking are all ways that the leader's personal style affects action in the district. Articulating core commitments effectively and maintaining a purposeful and consistent leadership style can go a long way to creating a solid foundation upon which district improvement can occur.

Perhaps the most important reason a superintendent should possess a high degree of self-awareness and self-knowledge is to ensure the best possible match between the district and the superintendent. A good match can pay dividends over time in several ways, especially as a superintendent builds a history of making decisions and engaging in actions that align with and reinforce his or her core commitments and leadership style.

Being consistent and clear in word and action about core commitments and leadership style also helps a superintendent recognize when his or her core commitments no longer serve the needs of the district. One of the most difficult aspects of leadership is to make decisions and perform tasks that conflict with one's core commitments and leadership style. That is, it is very hard to move a district forward in any meaningful way when the board and superintendent are at odds about issues in which core commitment inconsistencies and disagreements over "how to do the business of school" surface. In short, self-awareness and self-knowledge are critical for thriving in a leadership position and knowing if and when it might be time to seek a different position.

Having strong core commitments and a deep knowledge of one's personal leadership style has several other benefits as well. This self-awareness can help a district leader maintain consistency in leadership, and avoid the temptation to head in multiple directions or go for quick fixes that promise easy solutions to difficult problems, but rarely (if ever) produce any meaningful results. Strong convictions and a consistent leadership style provides leaders with a sense of doing things right and doing the right things, which can sustain leaders through difficult periods and help make self-reflection more transparent and provide leaders with a sense of reassurance.

Superintendents possessing strong core commitments and consistent leadership style provide the board, staff, parents, and the community with confidence in the leader's ability to lead, and a comforting sense of predictability in the approaches and techniques the leader uses. This confidence does not mean that there is always agreement, but it should mean that constituents understand the direction and focus of the leader's actions.

Strong core commitments and a consistent leadership style are also invaluable when there are conflicts between the board and superintendent. Board turnover often occurs on an annual basis, and there is no guarantee that board's and superintendent's core commitments that were aligned in the past will continue to be aligned into the future. A firm grasp on one's own core commitments enables a superintendent to honestly assess whether the match between the board and superintendent continues to be workable, or whether it is time to find a position where he or she can be more effective and where the match will enable the superintendent to move the district forward.

It is also important to know one's self in terms of being realistic about one's ego needs. Collins (2007) analyzes and discusses ego needs and leadership. In Collins' framework, leadership is presented on five levels. Level 5, the highest level of leadership, "builds enduring greatness through a paradoxical blend of personal humility and professional will" (p. 31). That is not to say that a Level 5 leader has no ego needs; rather, these leaders "channel their ego needs away from themselves and into the larger goal of building a great company" (p. 30). Recognizing and finding ways to satisfy one's own ego needs that benefit the organization (the district) is important in maintaining an open mind and willingness to learn new things from all stakeholders, including internal and external resources.

Know Your Constituencies

When discussing district leadership in general and superintendency in particular, considering the full range of internal audiences and external publics is critical to success. Internal audiences and external publics include an elected board, students, parents, teachers, staff, administrators, and community members. All of these stakeholders are served in the context of a governmental entity that must comply with federal, state, and local laws and which requires a high degree of transparency. The diverse stakeholders that the typical superintendent serves require that he or she must understand, connect, and synthesize all interests into one overarching, cohesive framework called the school district. A deep level of knowledge about the core commitments, values, and culture of these stakeholders is essential for effective leadership.

In order to best serve the board and community, a savvy superintendent continually assesses the climate and culture of school board politics. For new board members and superintendents, the first year in a district reveals the political dynamics and realities at work. Budget constraints, constituent pressures, staff issues and demands, student issues, and media requests are realities that both the board and the superintendent must address on a daily basis. Maintaining an appropriate connection to the schools and assessing/addressing the needs of students is a never-ending task for both the board and the superintendent.

A stakeholder group that should not be overlooked is the administrative team. A superintendent should understand the values and priorities as well as the strengths and weaknesses of the administrative team. An objective assessment of these key stakeholders is much like assessing the talent for an athletic team. Making this assessment and engaging in continual follow up provides the superintendent with valuable information regarding potential talent and support available for any contemplated operational or program implementation. Engaging in continual assessment also enables the superintendent to identify areas where an individual or group may need additional expertise or assistance to implement a given plan or initiative. This information can be very valuable when considering when and which external experts might be most beneficial to the district.

As much as possible, it is important for a superintendent to be aware about the climate, culture, and student needs of each school in his or her district. This knowledge could include information about the student population, the staff, and the neighborhoods surrounding the school. Knowledge about student achievement, instruction, and building operations can also provide insights about what is working well in each school and what it not.

Most states provide extensive performance reports on each district and each school, and most school districts have data retreats where instructional teams analyze test scores, learning trends, and other data. These retreats also provide needed instructional planning time for administrators and key teacher leaders, and can also be valuable in ascertaining whether and when an external expert might be a worthwhile investment in helping one or more schools in some way.

However, performance reports, test scores, and other quantitative data do not portray a school completely or accurately by any means. Regular school visits and contact with teachers and administrators can provide a superintendent with a very different and direct assessment of climate and culture that enhances (or is enhanced by, depending on your perspective) state and district quantitative data. Dr. Evert recalls:

> For the first 12 1/2 years of my superintendency, I visited each school once a month to check in with principals or assistant principals and see for myself how things were going. These visits were always unannounced and were not intended to put administrators on the spot; rather, they were intended to help me learn firsthand about what principals were facing and to provide guidance and coaching as appropriate. That is, these visits helped me stay connected with the schools and support the principals. Principals indicated that they looked forward to these visits. They were proud to highlight the good work going on in their schools and appreciated the opportunity to talk about issues that were immediately on their minds.

A final constituency that any superintendent must consider is the community, which by definition includes a wide variety of individuals and groups. A superintendent should have a deep understanding of the external publics that the school district serves. What are the values and needs of the community? How are conflicting values and needs evidenced among community populations? Is the community fiscally and/or politically conservative, liberal, or moderate? How has the community historically supported the school district? Finding meaningful answers to these and other similar questions can help the superintendent identify and address district issues and problems in ways that are consistent with community needs and values.

The reason that "know yourself and your constituencies" emerged as a general lesson is because external experts who have been the most successful in the district (including those discussed in this book) have been engaged with this foundational area well established. On occasion, especially during times of changing personnel on the board, this context has not always been so clear, and attempts to bring in external experts have failed. Dr. Evert recalls:

> There was interest on the part of several board members (and echoed by administration) to learn about ways to save money on energy usage in the district. Within the last four years, there was an energy specialist employed by the district who focused efforts on such activities as buying energy in bulk at reduced prices, and working with building construction and repairs to install the most energy efficient items possible. Due to budget cuts, this position was eliminated. I became aware of a national program that was financially guaranteed to save the district money on energy costs. The board president and I arranged to have these external experts come in and speak to a board committee about their program. However, when these experts gave their presentation to the board committee, there appeared to be significant resistance that went beyond critical questioning. Certain members of the board were very vocal in their opinions, wondering why external experts were needed to come and help us do this work. Their attitude was that "we can figure it out ourselves with our business department and the local energy company" (where one board member was employed). This event was part of an ongoing change in which board members were asserting their belief that their own expertise and experiences would be at the forefront of recommendations and decisions. This experience confirmed my understanding that the ways that I had formerly worked with the board were no longer well-received or effective.

Understanding self and constituencies helps a superintendent to recognize need and analyze available resources to determine whether the substantial investment in time and money is worth consideration.

DEVELOP A CLEAR AGENDA AND LONG-RANGE PLAN, AND STAY ON TASK

The superintendent's agenda and the district's strategic, or long-range plan are the components of an effective district direction. When considering whether or not to engage an external expert, it is important that the district have an identifiable plan of action that follows the district direction unless there is an extremely compelling reason to make amendments. Of course, a district direction is only as good as the district's ability to engage in following through on the long-range plan and agenda. The role of the superintendent is critical to ensure that discussion and action maintains focus on the agenda and long-range plan.

In order to use both internal and external resources most effectively, a superintendent should possess a clear, personal agenda for the district. This agenda is different than a long-range plan or strategic plan that is developed with a team of stakeholder representatives. An agenda is a personally developed set of three or four very general items that enable the superintendent to articulate his or her core educational commitments as related to the district in a succinct and meaningful way. These items comprise a platform of sorts for the school leader. They enable the superintendent to quickly ascertain whether, in the grand scheme of things, the superintendent, the board, and community are a good match initially and continue to be a good fit over time.

Dr. Evert recalls:

> My agenda throughout my 14 years as superintendent remained constant: to focus on improving student achievement, accepting and encouraging diversity among students and staff, and increasing parental involvement. Virtually all of my work in the district was tied to moving these three areas forward. I believed that by focusing on these three improvement areas, the district would make the most gains for students over time.

The strategic, or long-range plan, on the other hand, is developed by a team of stakeholders and drives decision-making regarding new and existing activities, programs, course offerings, and other implementations for period of time, typically five years. A great deal has been written about strategic planning in recent years. The National School Boards Association (NSBA) (2006) defines strategic planning as a continuous process of planning, assessing (both internal and external environments), analyzing relevant trends, and identifying those strategies most effective for the context.

Daggett (2008) writes about the need to include the "3Rs" (Rigor, Relevance, and Relationships) for all students in strategic planning. Senge (1990) encourages leaders to incorporate systems thinking in the planning process. He identifies the hallmarks of systems thinking, that people learn to understand the realities of interdependency and change. This better understanding enables people to deal more effectively with those factors that are determinative in shaping consequences. Sharratt & Fullan (2009) indicate that it is far more effective to focus on a small number of priorities and to do them well as opposed to getting spread too thin with commitments and resources.

It is interesting to note that the research findings in the mid-to late-2000s support the actions that were taken in the case-study district regarding the development and implementation of long-range plans in the mid 1990s and beyond. A solid and clear long-range district plan was developed by the superintendent and stakeholder representatives, which incorporated the three areas of focus (increase student achievement, accept and encourage diversity, and increase parent involvement) that the superintendent articulated in his agenda for district improvement.

This long-range plan was formally approved by the board and created the framework under which new ideas, programs, and initiatives were developed and implemented. As these ideas, programs, and initiatives were developed, the superintendent used formal and informal ongoing assessments to determine whether and what additional support and/or expertise were necessary to move developing plans to successful implementations.

The foundation of a clear superintendent agenda and a board-approved long-range plan provided the necessary structure for moving the district forward in a lasting and meaningful way and to consider engaging external experts to help with the process. The superintendent found that laying this foundation took about a year and a half to two years. Several factors contributed to this timeline, and other district leaders may find that it takes more or less time, depending on the stability of the district and the needs that require attention.

Factors contributing to this timeline included a very stable culture and climate under long-standing leadership (a former superintendent of 17 years), a cooperative board of education, and the fact that the school leader was a rookie superintendent who had served as a high school principal and central office director. All of these factors resulted in a very stable school culture under new leadership that had already done much of the foundational work building relationships with key stakeholders. In this environment, the new superintendent felt that he could get to work right away as a change agent.

The stable school culture and long-standing leadership provided excellent foundations for the new superintendent. For example, some of the initial groundwork to developing a district long-range plan had been done. The former superintendent had enjoyed a good working relationship with the local media and civic organizations, and the district was generally a source of pride to the community. However, the stability of the district also presented some challenges to a new superintendent.

A stable school culture also meant the entrenchment of long-standing beliefs and ideas about schools, education, and community, even as societal and demographic conditions were rapidly changing. For example, a variety of internal audiences and external publics, including some veteran teachers, administrators, board members, and community members were challenged with understanding and addressing the effects of several societal changes on education. Changes included fiscal and cultural issues, such as an increased poverty level and increased cultural diversity. Changes also included other issues, such as the technology revolution and generational differences.

A cooperative board endorsed the superintendent's agenda and supported the development and implementation of the long-range plan. Without this support and a reasonably high level of agreement regarding direction between the board and superintendent, it can be difficult to develop and implement a long-range plan. Part of the purpose of the long-range plan is to articulate what is important that the school district accomplish over a certain time period (typically up to five years). When interests and ideas are presented outside of the purview of the long-range plan, the plan is in place to provide checks and balances to the board and superintendent and to maintain district focus and action. When there is friction between a board and superintendent, the development of an agenda and long-range plan may take even longer, or may take more than one turnover in leadership to accomplish.

Of course, an agenda and long-range plan are only as good as they are followed. Part of the superintendent's role is to keep district priorities and needs in the forefront of all decision-making and to stay on task with the implementation of long-range plan objectives. One effective way to keep people on task (especially in meetings where digressions can sometimes occur) is the use of quick verbal messages to bring groups back to the work at hand. Dr. Evert recalls:

> Keeping meetings focused and on task was a continuing challenge throughout my superintendency. Often, meetings would involve a group of engaged, interested, enthusiastic stakeholders, and most of them had excellent ideas and input to share. However, a point would be reached where I began to feel uncomfortable with the amount of time an issue was being discussed, or how far away from the issue the discussion was headed. I had an internal norm that guided my determination about when a discussion had reached a point where it needed to be "re-centered." One of the ways I would re-center the discussion was to pause and then deliberately restate the basic questions regarding why we were meeting and how the outcomes of this meeting would affect district direction.

Marzano and Waters (2009) observe that it is important to use "memorable messages," or as Gladwell (2000) describes them, "sticky messages." While a superintendent may be passionate about an agenda and long-range plan, having immediate access to effective memorable messages may be somewhat more illusive. While we certainly do not advocate hiring an external expert for the express purpose of feeding superintendents sticky messages, a significant collateral benefit of most of the external experts described in this book is that they knew their area of expertise so well that they were able to help the superintendent drill down to the right memorable message that would keep efforts focused, help the district stay on task, and move the implementation forward.

PROFESSIONAL DEVELOPMENT FOR THE SUPERINTENDENT

The third foundational area that emerged from working with the external experts discussed in previous chapters is that superintendents should engage in regular, ongoing professional development that addresses their specific needs, whether it be conferences, coaching, courses, or other opportunities. The National School Boards Association (NSBA) (2006, p. 36) stresses the need for the board and superintendent to support professional development for all professionals in the district.

While little research has been done to formally link superintendent longevity to professional development, superintendent longevity is believed to have a positive impact on school districts. As Marzano and Waters (2009) have found, longevity is linked to learning and their findings suggest "that the longevity of the superintendent has a positive effect on the average academic achievement of students in the district" (p.9). The quality of educational leadership also seems to be tied to longevity. For example, most of the American Association of School Administrators 2009 Superintendent of the Year Forum Award recipients had been in their role as superintendent "longer than the average tenure of three years" (p. 6).

The personal experience of the authors also supports the hypothesis that an extremely important factor contributing to longevity and effectiveness throughout a superintendent's tenure is continuing and regular professional development. Superintendents, like any other professionals, need time to collaborate and associate with colleagues. They need to know best practices, approaches, programs, and other implementations that will help them improve their districts, and they need this information from the perspective of district leadership.

Superintendents need to consider new and innovative solutions to existing and persistent problems, and need to collaborate and learn from those who are experts in one particular area or another. The superintendent is often the key person in driving a district-wide implementation, and engaging in professional development on a regular and ongoing basis will help ensure that he or she is supporting implementations that align with long-range plans and have the best chances of achieving the desired outcomes.

Professional development for the superintendent, like professional development for teachers and other administrators, is an investment in quality outcomes. As such, it is reasonable to expect this investment to pay dividends. While it can be difficult to predict the return on investment for any particular professional development activity, some activities may yield significant results for the district (such as the adoption and implementation of a program or operational change), while others may help the superintendent do his or her job more effectively in less obvious ways.

One important return on professional development dollars for a superintendent is the relationship and network building with the top researchers and practitioners in various areas of education. For example, two of the external experts discussed at length in previous chapters were engaged to work with the district as a result of relationship and network building through professional development activities.

Engaging in professional development activities on an ongoing and regular basis has another important benefit for superintendents. Regular contact with colleagues and experts outside of the district boundaries develops the habit of reaching out to search for solutions to district problems and issues. While it is important to recognize and cultivate all of the internal resources available, certain issues and implementations need a greater level of expertise to achieve positive outcomes than are available internally.

It is easy for a superintendent to get very engrossed in the day-to-day operations and politics of a district, and to develop the mindset that everything can be solved, fixed, amended, or adjusted using internal means. Ongoing and regular professional development provides a superintendent with perspective and awareness of the resources that are available externally, and he or she will arguably be in a better position to decide when and for what issues it might be best to consider looking to external experts for guidance.

Superintendents typically have a wide variety of professional development opportunities through state and national organizations, and universities and colleges. Taking full advantage of these opportunities and seeking other, more unique opportunities for professional development can help the superintendent obtain and most effectively use external experts such as those discussed in previous chapters.

CONSIDERING EXTERNAL EXPERTS USING A FRAMEWORK BY MARZANO AND WATERS

After much discussion and analysis of what was learned from the six external experts discussed in this book, we decided that there would be value in conducting either a formal or informal "post hoc analysis." Many insights and observations shared throughout this book were not articulated or necessarily evident when work began on the manuscript. As the informal post hoc analysis continued throughout the writing of the book (including review of data, reflection, and discussion), it became evident that it would be very helpful to have a framework in place to use as we gained deeper understanding and began articulating our lessons learned.

Marzano & Waters (2009) created an excellent framework in their book *District Leadership that Works: Striking the Right Balance,* in which they provide leadership advice to superintendents. While this advice does not directly address the engagement of external experts per se, it has been very useful to use the advice provided by Marzano and Waters for reflecting on lessons learned about external experts. We believe five pieces of advice in particular transfer well to our analysis of lessons learned.

First, Marzano and Waters stress the importance of knowing the implications of new initiatives. In the context of engaging external experts, it is important to understand as much as possible about the political and educational consequences, both intended and unintended, of engaging a given expert. As targeted change agents, each of the experts discussed in this book had a significant impact on the district. Most of these impacts were planned and foreseen, and therefore carefully considered before the decision to hire the expert was made. However, some impacts on the district were unforeseen, creating unintended collateral effects.

Overall, these collateral effects were very positive. For example, Dr. Golarz not only helped to guide the district in the development of a new decision-making model, but also helped with the district's long-range planning efforts and served as an advisor to the superintendent. Ken Trump identified safety and security needs in the district that had not been previously identified, and the district was able to address these needs as part of the grant implementation.

Second, Marzano and Waters discuss the importance of the board and superintendent maintaining a united front (p. 8). When considered in the context of engaging an external expert, it is important that the board and superintendent are united in their support of the expert's work. The external expert should have this support regardless of the discussion and agreement/disagreement that may have occurred before a vote was taken or a final decision was made to engage the expert. That is not to say that the board and superintendent should not assess the work of the expert and provide ongoing feedback regarding the progress the expert is making; they should.

However, the work of the external expert should not be undermined or sabotaged by board members who did not want the expert hired in the first place. This scenario may result in a significant waste of time and resources, not to mention frustration for the external expert and the school district. This board/

superintendent support is particularly important when the expert is being engaged to address difficult issues or make significant changes that are sure to bring some challenges from teachers, principals, parents, or community members. For example, engaging in the difficult work of closing the achievement gap and providing more effective learning environments for an increasingly culturally diverse population in the case study district required that the board and superintendent support Dr. Odom's efforts in a united manner.

Third, Marzano and Waters encourage leaders to keep the big ideas in the forefront. In the context of engaging external experts, it is important that the superintendent and board are clear and consistent about why the expert is engaged. That is, it is important to keep the intended results and goals in mind and regularly communicate them to stakeholders. The messages used to convey big ideas should be accessible and worthy of regular repetition; that is, simple, but not necessarily simplistic.

For example, Dr. Odom was engaged "to help the district close the achievement gap between white and minority students." Ms. Wirth was engaged "to help the district improve its bond rating." Mr. Trump was engaged "to improve district and school safety in a world of twenty-first century threats." Clearly articulating these big ideas and keeping them in the forefront with staff, administration, the board, and the community provides a critical level of support and direction for the expert, and will help to maximize the expert's effectiveness.

A closely related fourth piece of advice that Marzano and Waters give is that it is important to use memorable messages, or as Gladwell (2000) described them, sticky messages. These messages go beyond keeping the big ideas in the forefront and are designed with the potential to create change. "Is it [the message] so memorable, in fact, that it can create change, that it can spur someone to action?" (p. 92)

Messages like "we need to close the achievement gap" convey a sense of urgency that is likely to spur action. Sticky messages like "remember Columbine" and "we live in a post 9/11 world" broaden traditional notions of school safety threats, and as a result, have changed the ways school districts approach school safety and coordinate efforts with first responders. When sticky messages are used in conjunction with big ideas, there should be little doubt in stakeholders' minds about why an external expert has been engaged and what his or her mission in the district is.

The fifth and final piece of advice borrowed from Marzano and Waters is that district leaders should effectively manage personal transitions during times of change. Marzano and Waters clarify this point with the phrase "change is external, transition is internal." In the context of external experts, leaders should understand that change facilitated by external experts likely requires some personal transitions for stakeholders.

The superintendent may need to manage his or her own personal, internal transitions, and may also need to help other stakeholders manage internal transitions to new thinking and new approaches as well. For example, when the Studer Group initiative began in the district, professional development time for the administrative team more than doubled. The philosophy of the old system was to allow principals and assistant principals maximum time during the school day to focus on operations in their buildings. Under the new system, training for administrators received a great deal more emphasis. As a result, principals and assistant principals spent significantly more time during the school day in professional development sessions.

Clearly, the approach of the Studer Group required a significant shift in philosophy. In order to adjust to this new approach, the superintendent underwent a personal transition. This transition was predicated on a struggle in addressing this question: How much time is the right amount of time for administrative staff development?

SPECIFIC LESSONS LEARNED

It would be remiss to discuss lessons learned without addressing some specific and concrete recommendations and reminders that proved to be helpful in achieving positive outcomes for the district through the use of external experts. This section focuses on specific and practical items. The recommendations and reminders are numbered; it is important to note that not every recommendation or reminder applies to every situation and context and the recommendations are not in order of the steps needed or importance.

RECOMMENDATIONS

1. *Have a budget for external experts.* A good rule of thumb is about three-tenths of one percent of an annual district budget. At the time the budget is presented to the board, the superintendent should consider laying the groundwork for reasons that he or she believes that an external expert might be helpful to the district. The superintendent should also be prepared for any scrutiny from the board, staff, media, and the public for such requests.
2. *Have a process in place for interviewing and hiring an external expert.* It is strongly recommended that the process be discussed with the board president and that the entire board be informed of (or involved in) progress and other general items throughout the hiring process. This process may require having a board policy in place.

3. *Follow the hiring process.* As with any individual employed in your district, check references carefully and conduct an extensive interview. It is very important to make sure you as superintendent have a high comfort and confidence level in the expert and that you are also comfortable with the board's confidence in the expert.
4. *Discuss details with the board and the external expert.* Be clear with the board and the external expert regarding salary, time commitments, documentation, program evaluation, external expert evaluation, and other contract arrangements. Send an extra copy of the contract or letter of agreement to the expert in advance of the visit.
5. *Prepare for the external expert's visits.* Once the work of the expert is underway, prepare an agenda with the expert one to two weeks in advance of the first contracted visit to the district.
    a. Be sure board members and administrative team staff are informed and updated on the logistics of the visit. Include the name of the host staff member (if applicable), arrangements for meals and lodging, to whom receipts for reimbursements are submitted, and other such details.
    b. Working lunches often fit best with board members' schedules. *If Board members are meeting with the expert, be sure to consider Open Meeting Law requirements.*
    c. Prepare a document for the expert outlining the details of his or her visit to the district. Include arrival times, host information, schedule of meeting, departure time, and other details. Find out whether the expert would like to tour the district/community in advance of, or as part of his or her first visit.
6. *Record the expert's time in the district.* Ensure accurate meeting minutes (including any necessary follow up) are taken and distributed after each session. It is helpful if the external expert provides a brief (typically one to two pages) summary of the visit. This summary should include a link to their overall purpose of working with the district/superintendent (e.g., safety, finance, leadership).
7. *Identify emerging issues.* Issues that emerge as a result of visits from an external expert often generate the need for follow up and can serve as the basis for next session's agenda.
8. *Update the board and key staff members.* Provide board members and key staff members with brief summaries and reminders of lessons learned and/or direction needed between sessions with the expert. The power and influence of the expert's message can be magnified through writing and verbal presentations at board and/or staff meetings.

9. *Establish channels of communication for the external expert.* Be clear about the channels of communication that the external expert is expected to use, and to whom the external expert reports. Board members, administrative team members, and/or staff should not be contacting external experts (or vice-versa) about district business unless the appropriate channels of communication are followed.

REMINDERS FOR SUPERINTENDENTS

1. There is no compelling guideline as to when a superintendent may wish to employ an external expert. The superintendent in this case study chose to engage an external expert after being in the district for a few years; however, the circumstances under which a superintendent is hired, his or her familiarity with the district, and his or her overall experience in leadership and education should all be considered when determining whether it is time to consider an external expert.
2. Consider a long-term partnership with the external expert. This consideration is important for the leader who wants to be a long-term superintendent in the district he or she currently serves. The importance of longitudinal knowledge and relationship building cannot be overstated.
3. Consider that an external expert may create major shakeups in customary norms of operation, including communications and order of authority.
4. Monitor reactions of various stakeholders on a regular basis regarding the expert's advice and performance. Effective monitoring may include formal and informal components, such as formal feedback surveys or informal discussions among leadership and key stakeholders.

Public schools mirror the society they serve. At the present time, public schools are under increasing pressure to raise student achievement levels for an ever-increasingly diverse population of students with a wide range of needs. Superintendents have important and challenging work in addressing the needs of these students under the overall direction of elected school boards. Big picture leadership and daily management of critical operations also involves regular and effective interactions with staff, parents, and the community.

Superintendents must seek resources in familiar venues, such as state, regional, and national associations, universities, and colleges. They should also seek out other resources that, if used correctly, can provide economical, effective, and lasting positive outcomes for districts. External experts are an important alternative resource that can be considered. The six external experts outlined in this book, using a single-district case-study approach, provided ideas and direction over the course of a 14-year tenure of one superintendent. These experts have had a very positive effect on the district in the following areas of expertise:

1. School governance and district decision-making
2. Minority student achievement
3. Understanding generational differences
4. School finance
5. School safety
6. Applying health care leadership systems to public education

These experts were chosen for their effectiveness in the district and because their area of expertise matched the district's area of need, not because there is anything uniquely special about their areas of expertise as opposed to other areas of expertise. Regardless of the area of need or area of expertise, the authors have learned a great deal through the process of reflecting, analyzing, discussing, and writing this book. Our primary lessons learned are reflected in the last chapter, including the importance of a solid foundation in three key areas (know yourself and your context, develop an agenda and long-range plan, and engage in regular and ongoing professional development), an analysis of lessons learned using a framework provided by Marzano and Waters, and a short list of specific recommendations and reminders.

Whether or not your district ultimately chooses to use an external expert, being aware of what they have to offer can be very important for competent superintendents. When addressing certain problems and issues, an external expert can be a very efficient and cost effective way to achieve positive outcomes for the district, especially during financially trying times. We believe that judicious and carefully considered use of external experts can help a district achieve continuous improvement for students, staff, administrators, parents, and the community.

References

AASA, (2009). Leadership for change. *AASA National Superintendent of the Year Forum.*

Adelman, H. S., and Taylor, L. (2006). *The school leader's guide to student learning supports: New directions for addressing barriers to learning.* Thousand Oaks, CA: Corwin.

Burke, P. (2009). *The elements of inquiry: A guide for consumers and producers of research.* Glendale, CA: Pyrczak.

Calhoun, E. (1994). *How to use action research in the self-renewing school.* Arlington, VA: Association for Supervision and Curriculum Development.

Collins, J. (2001). *Good to great: Why some companies make the leap . . . and others don't.* New York, NY: Harper-Collins.

Collins, J. (2007). Level 5 leadership. *The Jossey-Bass reader on educational leadership (2nd ed.).* San Francisco, CA: Wiley.

Cooper, D. J. (2009). Professional development: An effective research-based model. New York, NY: Houghton Mifflin. Retrieved from www.greatsourcerigbypd.com.

Creswell, J. (2009). *Research design: Qualitative, quantitative, and mixed method approaches.* Thousand Oaks, CA: Corsage.

Daggett, W. (2008). *Leading change in high schools: theory and practice.* Excerpt from unpublished manuscript. Retrieved from http://vaascd.org/BillDaggettHandout.pdf.

Danielson, C., and McGreal, T. L. (2000). *Teacher evaluation: To enhance professional practice.* Alexandria, VA: Association for Supervision and Curriculum Development.

Downey, C. J., Steffy, B. E., English, F. W., and Frase, L. E. (2004). *The three-minute walk-through: Changing supervisory practice one teacher at a time.* Thousand Oaks, CA: Corwin.

DuFour, R., and Berkey, T. (1995). The principal as staff developer. *Journal of Staff Development, 16*(4), 2–6. Retrieved from http://www.leaningforward.org/news/jsd/dufour164.cfm.

DuFour, R. (2007). In praise of top-down leadership. *The School Administrator, 10*(64), 38–42.
Editor, Wisconsin State Journal (2002, March 13). *Madison authors offer fresh outlook on race.* Wisconsin State Journal Editorial. Copy in possession of author.
Elmore, R. F. (2007). Professional networks and school development. *The School Administrator, 4*(64), 20–24.
English, F. W., and Steffy, B. E. (1984). *Educational consulting: A guidebook for practitioners.* Englewood Cliffs, NJ: Educational Technology.
Ehrhardt, K., and Sperry, S. (2009). *Rounding versus walk-through supervision.* Unpublished paper.
Gladwell, M. (2000). *The tipping point: How little things can make a big difference.* New York, NY: Little, Brown and Co.
Golarz, R. J., and Golarz, M. J. (1995). *The power of participation: Improving schools democratic society.* Champaign, IL: Research Press.
Golarz, R. J. (date unknown). *Some new tools.* Unpublished materials.
Haslam, B. (1997, Fall). How to rebuild a local professional development infrastructure. *NAS Getting Better By Design.* Arlington, VA: New American Schools.
Heath, R. (2009). *Celebrating failure: The power of taking risks, making mistakes, and thinking big.* Franklin Lakes, NJ: Career Press.
Howe, N. (2010). Meet Mr. and Mrs. Gen X: A new parent generation. *The School Administrator, 1*(67), 18–23.
Howe, N. (2005). Talking about their generations. *The School Administrator, 8*(62).
Howe, N., and Strauss, W. (1993). *13th generation.* New York, NY: Vintage.
Howe, N., and Strauss, W. (2000). *Millennials rising: The next great generation.* New York, NY: Vintage Books.
Hoyle, J. R., Björk, L. G., Collier, V., and Glass, T. (2005). *The superintendent as CEO: Standards-based performance.* Thousand Oaks, CA: Corwin.
Jenkins, L. (2008). It's the system (not the staff) that needs a tuneup. *The School Administrator, 4*(65).
Kafele, B. K. (2009). *Motivating black males to achieve in school and in life.* Alexandria, VA: Association for Supervision and Curriculum Development.
Keyser, D. R. (2010). *An inductive exploratory study of the effects of rounding for outcomes on school climate and leadership.* Doctoral Dissertation.
Lachman, A., and Wlodarczyk, S. (2011). Partners at every level: From the classroom to the boardroom, consultants work toward districts' goals. *Journal of Staff Development, 31*(1), 16–20.
Lindsey, R. B., Robins, K. N., and Terrell, R. D. (2003). *Cultural proficiency: A manual for school leaders (3rd ed.).* Thousand Oaks, CA: Corwin.
Lovely, S. (2010). Building an age-friendly workplace. *The School Administrator, 1*(67), 10–14.
Lunenburg, F. C., and Ornstein, A. C. (1996). *Education administration: Concepts and practices (2nd ed.).* Boston, MA: Wadsworth.
Marzano, R. J., and Waters, T. (2009). *District leadership that works: Striking the balance.* Bloomington, IN: Solution Tree Press.

McCabe, N. C., Cunningham, L. L., Harvey, J., and Koff, R. H., (2005). *The superintendent's fieldbook: A guide for leaders of learning.* Thousand Oaks, CA: Corwin.

National School Boards Association (2006). *Becoming a better board member: A guide to effective school board service (3rd ed.).* Alexandria, VA: National School Boards Association.

Odom, J. Y. (2001). *Saving black America: An economic plan for civil rights.* Sauk Village, IL: African American Images.

Odom, J. Y. (2008). *School district of Janesville analysis of human relations and diversity activities.* Memo to district.

Patterson, J. (1993). *Leadership for tomorrow's schools.* Alexandria, VA: Association for Supervision and Curriculum Development.

Riley, R. W. (1993). The emerging role of professional development in education reform. *On Common Ground.* Retrieved from http://www.yale.edu/ynhti/pubs/A14/riley.html.

Safko, L., and Brake, D. K. (2009). *The social media bible: Tactics, tools, and strategies for business success.* Hoboken, NJ: Wiley.

Senge, P. (1990). *The fifth discipline: The art and practice of the learning organization.* New York, NY: Doubleday.

Sergiovanni, T. J. (1996). *Moral leadership: Getting to the heart of school improvement.* San Francisco, CA: Jossey-Bass.

Sharratt, L. and Fullan, M. (2009). *Realization:The change imperative for deepening district-wide reform.* Thousand Oaks, CA: Corwin.

Strauss, W., and Howe, N. (1991). *Generations.* New York, NY: Quill.

Strauss, W., and Howe, N. (2006). *Millennials and the pop culture.* Great Falls, VA: Lifecourse Associates.

Strauss, W. and Howe, N. (1997). *The fourth turning.* New York, NY: Broadway Books.

Studer, Q. (2005). *101 answers to questions leaders ask.* Gulf Breeze, FL: Fire Starter Publishing.

Studer, Q. (2003). *Hardwiring excellence: Purpose, worthwhile work, making a difference.* Gulf Breeze, FL: Fire Starter Publishing.

Studer, Q. (2008). *Results that last: Hardwiring behaviors that will take your company to the top.* Hoboken, NJ: Wiley.

Ward, M. (2010). The long haul: The challenge to school reform is making improvements that endure. *American School Board Journal, 197*(9), 30–31.

Weick, K. (1995). *Making sense of the organization: The impermanent organization (Vol.2).* West Sussex, U.K.: Wiley.

Westchester Institute for Human Services Research, The (prepared by), (1998). Professional development. *The Balanced View, 2*(3), 1–5. Retrieved from http://www.sharingsuccess.org/code/bv/pd.html.

Wong, H. K. (2002). Induction: The best form of professional development. *Educational Leadership, 59*(6), 52–55.

Index

accountability, 15, 23, 66, 91, 106–108

board–superintendent relationship:
contentious, 31, 116, 122; dynamics, 2, 9, *21;* external experts, effects on, xiii, 106; participation and decision making, 55–57; politics, 81; risk taking, 105; student needs, 117; working together, 59, 59, 84, 125–26
budgets: cuts and tight budgets, xii, 108, 117; discretionary, 8, 13–14, 32, 63, 90; fund balance and, 81–84; funding options, 96, 127; hiring Odom, 63; hiring Strauss, 90; managing district wide, 51–53
Bunton, D., 81

Cappies, 89–90
case study approach, 2, 111, 126, 129–30
change agent, targeted, 10, 12, 19, 96, 112, 125
collaboration, 7, 66, 67
color green, 21, 63, 72–73
condition for debate, 34
consultants, vii, ix, 11, 25, 53–54, 61, 74, 87
consultation, 5, 14, 18, 73

contract with external expert, 16, 63, 99–100, 104–108, 129
cooperation, between districts, 15
Cooperative Educational Service Agency (CESA), 7, 93
costs: benefit: 14, 18; effectiveness, 13, 94, 129; fiscal implications, 40; general, 7, 11, 14, 18, 26, 96

decision making model. *See* participatory leadership
directors, 4, 81, 84, 97
diversity, cultural, *61–75*, 113, 120, 130
documentation, 16, 128
donation of services 105–106

economics. *See* color green
ego needs, 117
external experts:; advisor to the superintendent, 52; board of education, 14–15, 57, 82, 119, 125–28; changing roles, 51, 57–58; contracts, 16, 99, 107–108; defined, vii, 9; effect on superintendent, 73–74, 92, 98, 100; experience with, x, xiii, 3, 87; funding, 2, 4–9, 13–14, 26, 84–85, 100, 127; featured external experts, x, *18–24*, 96, 114,

135

129; general, xii; hiring, 14–15, 127–28; one-time visit, 90; professional development, *16–18*, 25; progress reviews, 74; skepticism toward, xii, 8, 10; term of service, 10
external resources, x, 2, 5–6, 17, 120, 124
Evert, T. *See* superintendent

federal grants. *See* Grants
funding for external experts, 13–14, 32, 63, 84, 86, 90, 100, 127

generational differences, 78, *89–93*, 130
good to great, 10–12
grants, 84–86, 95, 107–108

Heath, R., 11, 100

internal resources, 1, 4, 12–13, 27, 52, 96, 124

Jenkins, L., 101–102

leading from the back, 100

Marzano and Waters, 124–127

national perspective, external expert 19, 55, 87
n of one. *See* superintendent

parents: elementary strings, 46; generation X, 93; involvement, 32; schools need their support, 50
participatory leadership:; changes to, 37–38, 41–42; general, 21, 29, 37–45, 52, 55–58
partnerships, 6, 9, 70, 72, 99–100, 103, 105–109
Patterson, J., ix, 31, 97
principals: checks and balances, 58; core value assessments, 42–43; decision making, 21, 41, 57; diversity, 64; elementary strings, 46; importance, xi; not adversarial, 40; roles, 48
public engagement, 44–51, 58

questions to ask, 15–16

recruiting minorities, 63–64, 69–71
return on investment (ROI), 11, 124
risks, 13, 19, 33, 36–37, 43, 56

school board: approving funds, 12–15, 107; attendance at training session, 99; external experts' effects on, 57–58; board meetings, 45; board service, xiii, 117; board turnover, 116, 119; core value assessments, 36–38, 42–43; decision making, 33, 39, 47–48, 97; external experts, interactions with, xii–xiii, 10, 55, 78–84, 90, 101; funds, 16, 53, 90, 100, 107–108, 128; general, 12, 18, 35, 47 54, 59; informed of external experts, 63, 90; leadership, 97, 116; long-range plan, 105, 121–22; open meeting, 128; participatory leadership, 38–39, 44; professional development, 123; public engagement, 49–51; superintendent communications, 93–94, 104; superintendent leaving, 105; supporting external expert, 52–53; tension, 105, 122; Van Deuren, xii–xiii, 53, 86–87
school finance, 77–78, 95
school safety, 78, 84–89, 125, 130
servant leader, 17
social media, vii
status quo, 20, 97
sticky messages, 114, 122–23, 126
student achievement: achievement gap, 21, 62–63, 67, 73–75, 126 ; millennial generation, 91–92

superintendent: agenda, 114, 119–21; budgeting responsibilities, 13; change not linear, 44–45, 126–27; change process, 19, 25, 31, 56; climate and culture, 111–13, 121; diversity effort, 67–69, 72; early years, 29–31, 121; effects of external experts on, 61, 73, 92–93, 98, 100; Evert, T., ix–xii, 29–30, 33, 42–43, 51–52, 62–63, 72, 90–92, 94, 98–99, 100, 118–122; getting started with external expert, 15, 61, 89–90, 94, 99, 104, 106–108; later years, 53–54; leadership, general, 1–2, 58, 62, 98, 123, 129; leaving position, 105; match with board, 116; middle years, 62; *n* of one, 16–17; professional development, 12, 14, 16–18, 112, 114, 123–24; style and tasks, 115–19; systems perspective, 51–52; tenure, 3, 48, 114, 123

superintendent–administration relationship, 32–44, 47–48, 56–59, 91–94, 103

Superintendent's Advisory Committee, 30, 44, 47–48, 50

Superintendent–board relationship. *See* Board–superintendent relationship

system change, ix–x, 32

system flaws, 101

systems approach, xi, 51–52, 120

targeted change agents. *See* Change agents, targeted

urgency, 10, 61–62, 98, 100

values, assessment of core, 32–38, 42–43, 56, 59

Van Deuren, A. *See* school board

Wolfe, T., 53

About the Authors

Thomas F. Evert is a former public school superintendent of fourteen years and has served as a high school principal and director of student services. His doctorate is in Ed. Psych. from the University of Wisconsin–Madison. Dr. Evert is currently an instructor at Edgewood College in Madison, Wisconsin. He teaches courses in law, media, curriculum, and instruction in addition to serving as a doctoral dissertation advisor.

Amy Van Deuren is an educator and author, and has a law degree from the S.J. Quinney School of Law, University of Utah. She is currently an adjunct faculty member and internship supervisor at National Louis University, teaching courses in school law, school-community relations, finance, policy, and research. In addition, Ms. Van Deuren is an instructor at Edgewood College teaching school law.

www.ingramcontent.com/pod-product-compliance
Lightning Source LLC
Chambersburg PA
CBHW022015300426
44117CB00005B/202